Crash Course in Dealing with Difficult Library Customers

Recent Titles in
Libraries Unlimited Crash Course Series

Crash Course in Dealing with Difficult Library Customers

Shelley E. Mosley, Dennis C. Tucker, and Sandra Van Winkle

Crash Course Series

AN IMPRINT OF ABC-CLIO, LLC
Santa Barbara, California • Denver, Colorado • Oxford, England

Library of Congress Cataloging-in-Publication Data

Mosley, Shelley, 1950–
    Crash course in dealing with difficult library customers / Shelley E. Mosley, Dennis C. Tucker, and Sandra Van Winkle.
        pages cm. — (Crash course series)
    Includes bibliographical references and index.
    ISBN 978-1-61069-283-0 (pbk.) — ISBN 978-1-61069-284-7 (ebook)
1. Public services (Libraries)—United States.   2. Library users—United States.
3. Libraries—Public relations—United States.   4. Libraries—Security measures—United States.   5. Conflict management.   I. Tucker, Dennis C.
II. Van Winkle, Sandra   III. Title.
    Z711.M67   2014
    025.5—dc23   2013034584

ISBN: 978-1-61069-283-0
EISBN: 978-1-61069-284-7

18   17   16   15   14   1   2   3   4   5

This book is also available on the World Wide Web as an eBook.
Visit www.abc-clio.com for details.

Libraries Unlimited
An Imprint of ABC-CLIO, LLC

ABC-CLIO, LLC
130 Cremona Drive, P.O. Box 1911
Santa Barbara, California 93116-1911

This book is printed on acid-free paper ∞

Manufactured in the United States of America

To Vicki, Gary, and Steve—Mom always liked you best!
— Shelley and Sandy
To Dr. Jennie C. Cooper, Ph.D., for a lifetime of inspiration.
— Dennis

CONTENTS

ACKNOWLEDGMENTS

José Agiñaga, Suella Baird, Robin A. Boberg, Rachael Brown, Jennie Burrell, Vicki Burrell, Anna Caggiano, John Charles, Lisa Colcord, Krista Cornish, Susan Coronado, Kathy Coster, Carol Damaso, Dianne DeMeyere, Susan Drissi, Marion Ekholm, Mark Floor, Sylvia Fox, Jacque Gage, Stephen Hunter, Cynthia Johnson, Cheryl Kennedy, Greg Kinder, Sue Komernicky, Chris Larson, Shelly Larson, Sandra Lagesse, Cyndee Sturgis Landrum, David Mosley, Johan Nielsen, Ann Porter, David Rodriguez, Casey Van Haren . . .

And our intrepid editor, Blanche Woolls.

INTRODUCTION: A WORD ABOUT LIBRARY PATRONS

Good people do not need laws to tell them to act responsibly, while bad people will find a way around the laws.

—Plato (427 BC–347 BC)

Librarians aren't saints (except maybe St. Jerome, the patron saint of libraries). We moan and groan about the small percentage of customers we think of as problem patrons, who eat up our time, patience, and energy as though they were chocolate truffles. Trust us, when we surveyed other librarians, they had no problem coming up with a list of people with bad behaviors and attitudes for this book!

The hard truth is that most of our customers aren't problem patrons. However, during our long careers, with our combined experience of over 80 years in the profession, we've observed in many different libraries of various types (public, academic, and school) that certain behavior traits and personality types tend to repeat themselves. Public libraries especially, are, by nature, community gathering places. They attract a wide variety of people for a plethora of reasons and some have nothing to do with reading. Most people who visit their local library do so with the intention of being informed or entertained. They are courteous to the staff. They respect the facility and everything in it as a valuable, shared resource to be preserved for the benefit of everyone. They abide by the rules and honor library policies.

But every now and then, librarians encounter difficult customers who disrupt the library, its staff, and other customers. Even though this represents a small percentage of the library's patron base (some experts estimate 1% or lower), when your staff encounter these people, they need to know what to do. Untrained or undertrained staff members or volunteers can make a bad situation worse, especially when people who come into the library assume that every person working there (including the pages) is a "librarian" who has the immediate power and resources to solve their problems.

It's up to you, as the manager or supervisor, to ensure that your <u>entire</u> staff, from the pages to the professionals, as well as your corps of volunteers, knows what to do in these instances. There's a certain inevitability in dealing with the public. It's not a question of *if* problem patrons come to your library, but *when*, and you need to prepare for those eventualities. Most importantly, you need to lead by example.

It's vital to plan ahead and provide training for staff and volunteers to deal effectively with difficult customers. Each situation will have its own unique set of circumstances, so it's not only imperative to do that initial training, but also to have regular updates. Training should include:

- Reviewing written policies and procedures
- Reviewing which contacts to use (such as the police department) when problems accelerate
- Role-playing potential situations and the appropriate reactions to them
- Practicing active listening

When it comes to dealing with difficult customers, staff members have certain rights, including:

- You have the right to be in a safe, healthy work environment.
- You have the right not to be verbally abused.
- You have the right not to be threatened.
- You have the right not to be physically victimized or abused.
- You have the right to be in a nonhostile work environment.
- You have the right not to be sexually harassed or abused.

- You have the right to be in an open, nondiscriminatory workplace.
- You have the right to say no when a customer request falls outside the parameters of what is acceptable in a public environment.
- You have a right to ask someone to change his or her inappropriate behavior.
- You have constitutional rights.
- You have the right to full protection under the law.
- You have a right to dislike certain patrons. However, you do not have the right to give these people a lower level of service than you offer other customers. Your goal should be a consistent excellent service with a pleasant, professional attitude.

Staff members need to know that management supports them. One of the worst things a manager or supervisor can do is to contradict or reprimand an employee in front of a customer. If it's obvious the employee is in the wrong, the person in charge should quietly step in and intercede. After resolving the problem, the manager or supervisor should pull the employee aside, and, out of the hearing of other people, explain the proper procedure.

The types of difficult customers described in these pages are common to libraries everywhere. Librarians and other library staff will likely recognize most of them and can probably put faces to more than a few.

Dealing with problem customers can be challenging, and something many librarians dread. It requires tact, diplomacy, excellent listening skills, and above all, cool heads at a time when the customers may be losing theirs. Face it—most of us aren't Mother Teresa! Sometimes, when we deal with difficult customers, it takes every ounce of patience we have. And then some.

In writing this book, we're not trying to stereotype people or to poke fun at them. Rather, we intend to address certain types of behavior we have observed repeatedly in our many years of experience. These are real people and real situations. Only the names have been changed. Hopefully, some of our solutions to these problem behaviors will be helpful to you, our fellow library staff. In any case, we hope readers will see that they are not alone when it comes to dealing with difficult patrons.

PART I

Some General Guidelines in Dealing with Problem Customers

This book is intended to identify problem customers and propose some possible solutions in dealing with them. The next few chapters deal with specific situations, but here are a few general guidelines for dealing with difficult patrons:

Ask questions.

Never assume that you have understood. Listen carefully to their comments. Many times, a simple clarification is the key to solving a problem.

Avoid confrontation.

The surest way to escalate a situation is to be confrontational. Stay calm. Don't argue or dispute. Try to remember, the customers are *nearly* always right.

Be aware of what's going on in the library.

Walk around. Don't conduct yourself as though your bottom is glued to your desk chair. Is anyone acting strangely? Is there an adult lingering alone in the youth department? Are there kids or teens clustered around a computer screen? Be conscious of each situation, and try to determine why it exists, and whether it could become a potential problem.

Concentrate on what they're saying.

What words are they using? *How* are they saying them? Don't jump ahead and think about what your next sentence will be. Stay in the now.

Consider cultural differences.

One of the beauties of our country is its diversity. However, this means you will encounter different languages and different levels of English proficiency. This can lead to misunderstandings and frustration on both parts. Taking the time to become familiar with the diversity of your community and the cultures of your customer base will not only be greatly appreciated, but will help avoid potentially embarrassing, if not offensive situations.

Establish a bank of interpreters, people you can call when you need help with translations. Good sources might be other patrons, cultural organizations such as a Chinese Community Center, or language instructors from local high schools or community colleges. These volunteer interpreters don't have to come from the library world; they just need to be fluent in the language you need.

Language is not the only cultural difference. Cultural differences are engrained from childhood and are part of how people communicate. Personal space varies from culture to culture. Some cultures seem more excitable, some more withdrawn. Some cultures use sweeping hand gestures when they speak. Widely accepted figures of speech don't always make sense from one culture to another, and similar gestures can have very different meanings. To say "I think we got off on the wrong foot" may make absolutely no sense to someone unfamiliar with that colloquialism, and making a harmless, friendly gesture like a thumbs-up or a peace sign could trigger an international incident in some cultures.

Continue to offer great customer service.

This isn't easy when someone's in your face saying bad things about you or your library, and disrupting others. Consistently great service leads to fewer problems and nasty encounters.

Document. Document. Document.

Record incidents. (See Appendix A.) Use as much detail as you can remember, including witnesses, time, date, and place. A running record of incidents is invaluable, especially in cases where the problem is ongoing, or where different staff people have had difficulties with the same person. In some organizations, if it isn't documented, it didn't happen.

Don't stereotype.

Wholesale stereotyping spells disaster in any situation. As a manager or supervisor, you should be sure your staff is sensitive to cultural differences and doesn't treat people wearing the traditional clothing and accessories of their cultures differently than anyone else. A zero tolerance policy for racism and bigotry needs to be established and enforced for both staff and volunteers.

Stereotyping can lead to a fear of anyone who dresses differently than mainstream America. For example, teens and young adults use style and appearance as a means of self-expression and rebellion. The reasons may not be understood, but the young customers themselves should be accepted. Just because they're dressed in clothing mandated by the latest fads or have piercings and tattoos doesn't mean they're in the library to hurt you.

Don't think of the customer as an interruption.

This isn't always easy. With lowered funding and staffing cuts, we often find ourselves working at the reference desk while trying to order books, plan programs, or develop bibliographies. However, the public is our business, our *raison d'être*. Customers, good or bad, are why we're here. The people standing in front of you, even those who are cranky or angry, should be treated as valued customers. Greet them politely, even if they're being rude.

Establish win-win strategies ahead of time.

Compromise. No one needs to be a loser.

Know when to be quiet.

Adlai Stevenson once said, "In quiet places, reason abounds." It's still good advice.

Listen, listen, listen.

"Be a good listener. Your ears will never get you in trouble." These words of wisdom from erudite cartoonist Frank Tyger can prevent a world of difficulties. Try to hear the problem through the customer's ears. Develop the skill of good listening. Know when to be quiet. Let the customers air their concerns, and then rephrase what they've said after you've listened carefully, and then repeat it back to them. Practicing active listening is a great way to avoid misunderstandings.

Maintain your professionalism.

When angry or frustrated customers approach you, be polite. Introduce yourself. Maintaining a calm, professional demeanor should be the cardinal rule at all public desks in the library. This is also paramount when controlling conflict, whether dealing with problem customers or fielding simple complaints. A calm, constructive approach to problem-solving often elicits a similar response in return. It defuses anger and builds a cooperative relationship. Don't get defensive and begin arguing. Demonstrating a sincere interest in satisfying customers' concerns indicates they are appreciated and valued. Growing up, you might have been told the age-old adage, "Don't stoop to their level." Or perhaps you were told, "Kill them with kindness." Well, maybe Mom was right.

Make, and keep, eye contact with the other person.

Looking at your watch or glancing at some distraction over the person's shoulder are good indications that you're really not paying attention. "The eyes are the windows to the soul." Make sure yours are pointed at the people talking to you.

Pay attention to body language as well as facial expressions.

Furrowed foreheads, crossed arms, tapping feet or fingers, tight-lipped expressions, squinting, eye-rolling, hands on hips . . . the list goes on and on. Each one of these is a clue as to what the person is actually feeling. Body language is expressed from head to toe. In the process of communicating, people tend to say as much with their body as they do with their words, and often without realizing it. Subtle movements, the amount of eye contact, facial expressions, stance and even spatial proximity can reveal far more about a person's frame of mind than their words convey. Being alert to nonverbal cues is essential to controlling the tone of the conversation and allows you to keep the dialog constructive and on friendly terms.

Pay attention to your own body language.

Are *you* frowning? Are *your* arms crossed? Crossed arms mean you're closed to their ideas. This, and other defensive postures, can exacerbate a bad situation. Are you rolling your eyes? Do you appear open and receptive, or do you just appear annoyed that they've bothered you? Be mindful of your own body language to ensure you aren't sending messages that contradict the concern and sincerity your words are trying to convey.

Put yourself in the patrons' place.

Try to see the situation through their eyes. Why are they upset? What are they trying to accomplish and what obstacle(s) have they encountered?

Respect both internal and external customers.

It doesn't matter if the customer is from your organization or from the general public. Everyone we deal with, including our coworker, is a customer, and should be treated thusly.

Respect the customers' space.

Don't step toward people when they're complaining. No one likes to be crowded. Invading personal space may be construed as intimidating, aggressive, and confrontational, and rarely goes unchallenged. Provoking anger makes problem solving nearly impossible, and the backlash could possibly endanger staff and customers. Keep a respectful distance.

Respond consistently.

Do you really think people don't talk to each other about the library? Think again. For example, the practice of waiving a fee for some people and not others will eventually be communicated throughout the community, and your credibility will take a nosedive.

Respond quickly.

Nothing says, "I don't care" more than telling someone you'll look into their problem within the next 24 or 48 hours, or worse yet, when you have "enough time." You have just communicated to them that, as far as you're concerned, they are a very low, if not the lowest, priority.

Treat people the same way you want to be treated.

Most people know the Golden Rule. Some customer service experts have upgraded the concept of the Golden Rule to the Platinum Rule: "Treat others the way THEY want to be treated."

REMEMBER:
HOW <u>YOU</u> REACT TO ANY GIVEN SITUATION IS UP TO <u>YOU</u>. DON'T LET THE SITUATION CONTROL HOW YOU BEHAVE!

PART II

Patrons with Disruptive Behaviors

Moaners, Groaners, and Other Cranky People

ANGRY PATRONS: CAUSTIC COMPLAINERS

An angry man opens his mouth and shuts his eyes.

—Cato

How many times have you heard comments like these: "The librarians at the other library are so much better." "Do you people actually get paid with <u>my</u> tax dollars?" "Of course you didn't do anything about my suggestion; all you do is sit around and read books!" (Don't we wish?)

Caustic Complainers tend to find flaws, real or perceived. If something doesn't meet their specifications after they've asked to have it changed, they will often get angry. Always remember that Angry Patrons feel justified, and there is no anger stronger than righteous anger.

A common complaint from our Angry Customers is that the library doesn't have enough copies of a current bestseller to allow them to check out that title immediately. You too have probably dealt with this complaint. As library budgets continue to shrink, you can be sure these complaints will increase. Ensuring that your staff is well trained in reader's advisory helps, but until your ratio of requests to books is one-to-one, you will never satisfy everyone.

Some Enraged Complainers attribute their personal, sometimes absurd, inconveniences or problems to your alleged failures. One of our recent complaints was "I bought a crappy air conditioning unit because you didn't have the latest issue of *Consumer Reports*." At first hearing, this sounds ridiculous, but the patron was very agitated when he came in, and he really did blame us. We listened as he vented. And vented. And vented. When he ran out of steam, we told him we understood, and that we also use periodicals such as *Consumer Reports* as a guide to our own shopping. We apologized for not having the current issue available and suggested he contact his dealer since his unit was still under warranty.

Angry Customers can be loud and belligerent. It's hard, but don't take the tone or the complaint personally. By all means, don't launch a counterattack. This will only worsen the situation. Although you may feel tempted to get in a good shot of your own, don't do it. Your terse response will only make the already angry customer furious. Take a deep, calming breath, and try to remain unruffled. Resist the urge to fight back, and exude professionalism instead.

To paraphrase an old adage, other people can't make you angry, you allow yourself to become angry. Your anger will only make your customer's ire worse. Don't give a customer a reason to complain about <u>your</u> bad attitude. It's like Ambrose Bierce, a 19th-century journalist and satirist observed, "Speak when you are angry and you will make the best speech you will ever regret."

Think before you talk. Don't give a defensive, knee-jerk reaction to the complaint. Use empathetic words of concern and understanding, and keep your tone controlled and even. Sometimes, the only thing Angry Customers want is to have someone listen to what's making them cranky and cross. Try to put yourself in their place. This is often hard to do, but at least give it a try. After listening carefully and being sure that you understand their complaint, propose options, or suggest they put their grievance in writing.

Complaints must be dealt with promptly, both to reach an amicable solution and to keep the complaint from escalating into an angry tirade. After listening patiently, not to be confused with patronizingly, ask your Angry Customers what you can do to make it right. This indicates the willingness on your part to compromise, and tells them their complaint is important to you. As long as they're engaged in constructive conversation and can see progress, anger becomes less of the equation.

Some librarians are allowed to explain to their customers the overall budgetary problems that lead to such things as shortages of bestsellers for the customers. These librarians can suggest the customers contact the library's funding authority, for example, their city councilmember. Politics vary from city to city or town to town; sometimes city or town policies, written and unwritten, prohibit staff from telling a customer, "You're right. We don't have enough copies of bestsellers. We need a bigger book budget. You should call your councilmember and tell them the library needs more money." As much as you'd love to say this, in some jurisdictions, you have to bite your tongue.

Keep a supply of comment forms and pens or pencils visible and accessible. Even if your Angry Customers haven't already asked for a complaint form, offer to provide them with comment cards. Unless the complaints are completely irrational, you're likely to gain vital insights that can improve your customer service. Be sure to respond to all of them, whether they're comments, suggestions, or complaints, and do this in a timely manner.

Many complaints are valid. Correct the problems that led to the complaints. See the complaints as opportunities for improvement. Follow up with patrons once their complaints have been resolved, or at least properly addressed. Thank them for letting you know there was a problem. If their recommendations aren't feasible, let them know this, too. They can appreciate that you've at least tried, and it will save possible accusations of staff indifference in the future. Lack of follow-up will escalate feelings of anger, and there's a chance complaints will be taken to a higher level, meaning the mayor, city council, or town or city manager. Worse than this, a lack of follow-up shows a general apathy toward your patrons.

Don't foist Angry Complainers off on another staff member. An exception to this would be when there is no satisfaction in sight, or when the complainer insists on going to your supervisor or manager. If you happen to be the manager, <u>you</u> are where the buck stops.

If possible, move yourself and the Angry Customer away from the public area. To defuse anger, find a private, but not isolated, place where the individual can be allowed to vent. Be sure it's not so private that if a person becomes violent, you're cut off from help. Often, getting complaints off their chests is the best way for customers to return to calmer behavior.

Establish a buddy system. If customers are extremely agitated, other staff should watch and assist, if needed. Adopt a code name you can use if you require help, for example, "Mr. Dewey" or "Elsie Smith," and be sure all staff members and volunteers know that it means "security alert."

With patience, excellent listening skills, and prompt follow-up, you can generally calm the most furious customer. You can diffuse most situations. Who knows? You might even make that Angry Customer an ally. It happens.

In Summary

Irate Patrons and Caustic Complainers tend to find flaws or what they believe are flaws and feel justified in their anger. Even though they may be loud and abrasive, don't take it personally or allow yourself to argue with them. Keep your tone even, and try to see their point of view. Don't pass them from person to person, because this just escalates the situation. Encourage them to fill out comment forms. Be sure to follow up on them and communicate the outcomes with the customers.

BOTTLENECKS: INDECISIVE/FORGETFUL PATRONS

> To be, or not to be: that is the question . . .
>
> —William Shakespeare, *Hamlet* III.i.58

It happens to all of us, a case of indecision or a momentary lapse that causes us to hold up the line. We're all prone to some degree of bottlenecking; but the customers who are chronic bottlenecks cause us heartburn, like grocery shoppers who forget to rummage through their coupon collections until they reach the cashier. Or fast food customers who agonize over choosing thin crust or deep dish, or ask what "honey mustard" tastes like after they've tried the other nine flavors. Face it. Where there are people, there are bottlenecks. In the library environment, it takes patience and creative problem solving to minimize the effects of bottlenecks, keep the lines moving, carry on the flow of information, and ensure the other customers in line are happy.

Many customers approach the circulation desk fully prepared for checkout, with their items in order and their library cards drawn and ready to use. Some arrive juggling armloads of books, videos, and other media, only to announce they've lost their card and need a new one. Meanwhile, the line comes to a screeching halt, and the resulting wait causes long faces and short tempers among the inconvenienced patrons stacking up behind them.

Librarians are only human. Long lines may cause you to hurry and make mistakes. If possible, designate a special line or a "step-aside area" for those needing library cards.

Preventing long delays for service is essential for keeping patrons content and making their visit to the library enjoyable. The obvious solution for bottlenecks is assigning additional staff to the circulation or reference desks. This becomes an impossibility if your budget has been reduced and your personnel numbers are dwindling. Working within staffing limitations calls for a more creative approach.

Grocery stores do it. Hardware stores do it. Now, many libraries do it too. Self-service checkout stations are becoming more popular, and although they're not meant for complicated transactions, they do provide an option for customers who simply want to check out a few items and be on their way. At some self-check stations, it's even possible for customers to renew items and pay fines. This frees the circulation desk staff to focus on customers who have other business to conduct and who are prepared to accept a bit of a wait.

Adequate signage helps remind customers to prepare their items and their cards ahead of time for fast, seamless transactions. Adding a table or other working surface near where the line forms enables patrons to sort and organize their items and frees up their hands to fish out their cards while they wait. The U.S. Post Office does this very well. Why not the library?

Today, people of all ages are accustomed to the high speed and instant information available on the Internet. While the ability to conduct research at home is convenient, people know that a trip to the library is still the best way to access a variety of free, consistently reliable reference materials, not to mention the array of entertainment media. Guaranteeing that their visit is both fruitful and efficient encourages people to continue using and supporting their local library.

Some customers make quick trips to the library knowing exactly what they're looking for, and with no plans, or time, for browsing. The self-service stations are ideal for ensuring this type of patron a fast, easy, no-hassle transaction. Encouraging customers to take advantage of the library's online services enables them to reserve items ahead of time so staff can have the items ready and waiting for the customer's arrival. It also allows customers to search the online catalog instead of calling the library for title availability. Of course, customers who may not have access to the Internet are always welcome to call their library for information.

We've all assisted patrons who know exactly what they're looking for, except they can't recall the author's name or the book's title. Finding "that book about horses with the picture of a horse on the cover," doesn't give a librarian much to go on. Focusing on the information instead of the cover broadens the search to include more titles, and, in browsing through them, the "one" with the horse on the cover is likely to emerge. Customers might even be surprised to find one of the other titles is more useful. Effective bibliographies, a well-stocked reference desk, and a collection-savvy reference staff keeps the information flowing and the line moving. In an ideal world, there's room and staffing for separate reference and circulation desks; but sometimes this is neither feasible nor affordable.

It's difficult for patrons to be organized and efficient with restless little ones, ringing cell phones, and other interruptions all demanding their attention. Even in the relatively quiet confines of a library, life happens, and it's usually noisy and messy. Keeping simple, inexpensive distractions handy, such as colorful bookmarks for impatient children, can buy just enough time to complete the checkout transaction uninterrupted. Establishing and enforcing a policy for silencing cell phones inside the library is a simple way to maintain the peace and keep everyone focused.

For some patrons, a well-stocked library actually creates a dilemma. The large selection can make it difficult to decide which items to choose, especially knowing that the number of items eligible for checkout on a single topic may be limited. This indecisive patron can create a bottleneck at the reference desk. Directing customers to the appropriate section for browsing allows them to size up the collection and begin to sort through potential checkout items. Staff can help narrow their searches by offering suggestions of titles that might best fit their particular need. By knowing the collection and asking topic-specific questions, staff can help make the decision process a more efficient and enjoyable experience.

Some patrons make full use of their libraries, checking out stacks of books for the kids, a variety of videos and a handful of games, topping it off with a few items for mom and dad. These high-volume users help to keep the collection moving and circulation statistics high. Their continued patronage is healthy and encouraging. However, not everyone comes prepared to carry around this bounty. Keeping a supply of plastic grocery bags handy at the circulation desk and recycling them as book bags may not be glamorous, but it's convenient, inexpensive, and always appreciated, especially during inclement weather. Some libraries sell cloth bags emblazoned with their logos. This can be done either at cost as a convenience, or with a small profit for additional revenue. Making it easier for these patrons to carry their items saves everyone's time: that of the staff, as well as that of the patrons waiting next in line.

In Summary

If your library has lines of people, there are bound to be Bottlenecks. Whether these customers are indecisive, disorganized, or just plain forgetful, they will cause a delay in service for the other people there. Hiring more staff is not always possible. Other solutions at the circulation desk, such as self-check stations, step-aside areas, tables by the circulation desk, and adequate signage might cost money, too; but they're not as expensive as more personnel. To alleviate bottlenecks in the reference area make sure you have a collection-savvy staff that is thoroughly trained in research methods and databases, as well as reader's advisory services. This will shorten search times and make the search itself more efficient. Effective bibliographies are also good for browsers who are looking for good reads.

BRATS: THE RUNNING-TO-THE-OTHER-PARENT PATRONS

Liar, liar, pants on fire.

—Children's saying

If you have children, you've experienced this scenario before. You tell them "no," but they don't like your answer, so at the first opportunity they run to the other parent, hoping for a "yes." Sound familiar? Sometimes adults exhibit this same behavior in the library.

Brats play one staff member or one branch against another. They exploit weaknesses or omissions in your library policies, which they seem to have an uncanny ability to hone in on. To get their way, they may even outright lie about what another employee did or said. For example, a Brat might claim, "the other branch lets me keep my videos as long as I want." You know this isn't true unless they have a friend working at the circulation desk who gives them preferential treatment (which should be dealt with). You may be tempted to say, "this is <u>not</u> Netflix," or even question their honesty. Don't do either.

The most effective means to settle customer disputes is through dialog, which is not the same as arguing. Invite customers to explain their side of the dispute first, which they will probably be glad to do, sometimes at considerable length. Listen carefully, focusing on their side of the dispute instead of thinking about what you're going to say next. You will have time for that when it's your turn to speak. Meanwhile, interject attentive phrases like, "I didn't know that. I'll be happy to verify that for you." This indicates your willingness to reach an agreement, but also establishes that you want to be fair to everyone involved. Reach for the phone and call the other branch to ask about this new, unlimited checkout policy. When customers are merely trying to beat the system, this action forces them to rethink their position and allows them the opportunity to back out without embarrassment. When customers maintain their disputes, you have the full weight of the library's established policies behind you. Be fair, be consistent, be professional.

When your employees become the targets of Brats, it is your responsibility as their supervisor to back them up. Properly trained employees will know the library's policies and should be diligent in enforcing them. Your support of their decisions is important to maintaining unity among your staff and sends a clear message to Brat patrons that your staff will not be manipulated.

Sometimes the temptation to bend the rules "just this once" is difficult to resist. Certain patrons can be very convincing and their circumstances may even seem to justify making an exception. Don't do it unless there is clearly a reason to do so. Like feeding a stray cat, do it just once and they'll be back for more. This is doubly problematic if you overrule an employee's decision to enforce library policies and allow rules to be broken. Your disrespect will not go unnoticed by either the employee or the patron, and you'll be creating a potentially mushrooming problem for all of your employees. Like the old shampoo commercial, the Brat will tell two friends, and they'll tell two friends, and so on and so on.

If the Brat happens to be correct, that another branch does make exceptions and is inconsistent in enforcing library policies, take action immediately to resolve this internal issue. The library system only works properly if all policies are uniformly enforced and customers are treated equally. If this needs improvement, consider conducting a policy refresher course for all employees to ensure everyone understands the rules and enforces them in the same way. Frequent meetings with circulation staff with lots of room for input from those on the frontlines as to what works and what doesn't help keep everyone uniform and avoid problems before they occur. If possible, include the pages and volunteers, who also interact with patrons and will likely be asked for information. As part of the training, provide examples of how inconsistent policies affect customers, disrupt services, and create myriad problems for staff. Sometimes doing someone a favor just isn't worth it. We recently had a patron who was blocked because she owed the library a large amount in fines. She begged to use the library's Internet "just this once" to apply for a job. She worked her way from desk to desk until she found a staff member who felt sorry

From *Crash Course in Dealing with Difficult Library Customers* by Shelley E. Mosley, Dennis C. Tucker, and Sandra Van Winkle. Santa Barbara, CA: Libraries Unlimited. Copyright © 2014.

for her and, in violation of library policy, gave her a temporary pass. Doing so removed any motivation to pay her fines and set expectations that other staff members would unblock her account in the future.

Always give customers the benefit of the doubt and be careful to not embarrass them, even if the circumstances are self-inflicted. A bad experience at your library, regardless of who's at fault, could mean the loss of a patron and that person's friends and family. It's a ripple effect you want to avoid, so let the facts speak for themselves and react accordingly.

Like their young counterparts, Brats don't like to be told "no." Your refusal to break the rules could result in a customer complaint leveled against you or your staff, attacking your behavior and the way you handled the dispute. For this reason, remaining calm and professional throughout the encounter is extremely important. Always document the incident, particularly if it becomes contentious. Keeping a customer complaint log is a quick and easy way to track the types of complaints your library receives and record the outcomes. Remember: in some organizations, if it isn't documented, it didn't happen! This record should be kept secure and confidential. However, it can be a very useful customer service tool, revealing areas where improvement may be needed, making a visit to your library a more rewarding experience for everyone.

In Summary

Brats run from staff member to staff member or even branch to branch to get the answer they want. If they don't get the response they're looking for, they might even lie. Policies and procedures should be clear and uniformly enforced. Make sure staff knows, understands, and follows them. Listen to the Brat customers and remain professional. If they lie, don't accuse or confront them. Rather, use a phrase such as, "I didn't know that. I'll look into that for you." Whenever possible, use dialog to settle disputes, and if the conversation escalates into outbursts and threats, be sure to document it.

CHRONICALLY OVERDUE PEOPLE: ONLY IMAGINING REAL TIME

A diller, a dollar,
A ten o'clock scholar,
What makes you come so soon?
You used to come at ten o'clock,
But now you come at noon.

—Children's nursery rhyme

Edna's a nice person. She's pleasant to your staff. She even helps out when you're short handed. You like her. Edna's been coming to your library for 20 years, and since Day One, she's never turned anything in on time. She's never upset by her overdue fines. In fact, she's downright cheerful when she pays them, commenting that she hopes the money goes for more books.

So what's the big deal? Every day that Edna keeps a book or any of the other popular new materials of which she's so fond, and this is after she's used every allowable renewal period, another patron loses access. In this era of automated catalogs, library customers have learned to look in the record for an item's due date. They expect that book, magazine, CD, or DVD to be back to the library on the appointed day. When it doesn't appear according to schedule, they become frustrated, irritated, and/or angry, and you and your staff can be the recipients of their deservedly cranky attitudes.

The consequences for overdue items vary wildly from library to library. The severity runs the gamut from no overdue fines at all, to collection agencies, to arrests for long-term overdue offenders. Some libraries have a day or week of amnesty. Some collect cans of food for a food bank as "payment in full." Depending on local restrictions and the counsel of your board, you may be able to get creative about amnesty. For example, the San Francisco Public Library had a month of amnesty, during which they aired funny celebrity videos, "What's Your Excuse?" If there are no celebrities in your community, you could do the same thing with local figures, such as the school principal, fire chief, or mayor.

If you decide overdue penalties are absolutely necessary, or in this tight economy, you're relying on overdue fines as a revenue stream, there are still many decisions to be made. For example:

- What method(s) can people use to pay their overdue fines? Do you accept credit cards? Debit cards? Personal checks?
- Do you allow people unable to pay to work off their debts by doing such tasks as cleaning books or picking up loose materials in the library?
- Do you offer an installment plan or other payment arrangements?

And then there are overdue reminders:

- How often do you send them?
- How many reminders are sent?
- At what interval?
- Have you considered texting and emails to save postage? For this one you must remember that not everyone has access to the technologies necessary for these delivery systems.
- Does your library computer system feature automated telephone reminders?

Some agencies will handle patrons whose fine levels reach a certain threshold, whatever amount is set by the library. Based on the librarian's preference, these agencies may concern themselves only with the return of seriously overdue materials, or they may collect both fines and materials. These agencies are not the same as a collection agency in that items are not reflected on the customer's credit report. Rather, they are an intermediate step that can be used before credit-reporting customers.

Some librarians work with their local governments to send out invoices for library fines and overdue materials. For example, some librarians, in cooperation with the local public utilities division, add delinquent library information to the water bills. Of course, to take advantage of this situation, your customer service areas must match, and many logistical details will need to be worked out.

When items are chronically overdue, it may be helpful to find out if there are extenuating circumstances. Some customers may have a learning disability, be newly literate, or have a medical or psychological disability that makes them slow readers. Some librarians have created a "special borrower" type to give these customers an extended loan period. You also need to take into account fires, floods, and other disasters, which can lead to wholesale destruction of borrowed library materials. You need to have a written policy defining whether you will hold customers responsible under such conditions.

Back to our patron, Edna. You can't make a policy that applies only to one person—even if you like her. A couple of gentle reminders about other people waiting for the materials she's checked out may solve the problem. If your official policies demand stricter measures, limit the number of materials she can check out until all of her overdue materials are returned and paid for. You might even deny her access to circulation until the items are brought back and fines are paid. Some librarians have vastly improved their late returns by limiting or blocking access to library computers until patrons take care of all obligations.

No matter what you decide, you should have clear policies in place, and enforcement should be fair and consistent. Customers should be reminded verbally at checkout when their materials are due, and this should be followed with some sort of slip produced by the computer, unless your library isn't automated yet, and then checkout cards or even a simple bookmark will do the trick.

Don't be obsessed with overdues. Collecting fines is not your main function as a librarian but it's not something you can ignore either. Find a balance that will be fair to all involved.

In Summary

Whether they realize it or not, Chronically Overdue Customers affect others who are waiting for library materials. Consequences for overdue materials vary greatly. Once your policies are in place, make sure staff is consistent and fair about enforcing them. Make fines easy to pay. Many libraries are adding credit card payment capabilities for that very purpose. However, don't focus on fines! You're in the business of providing quality library services, not collecting money.

CLINGERS: STUCK TO YOU LIKE GLUE

It's no fun being lonely.

—Maurice Sendak

How often do you hear people say, "I love books! I should have been a librarian"? You can almost see their vision of what you do, sitting around and reading the entire day, chatting with customers, and then disappearing into that mysterious "employees only" area, where you lounge and relax, recovering after all that reading and chatting.

Most library customers respect their librarian's time, knowing the job involves a lot more than the small part they see. They notice how hard you work, especially during slow economic times, when budgets and staff are downsized, leaving fewer people to tackle the same workload; cover the circulation and reference desks; keep the collection shelved and the copier working; perform collection development tasks, write bibliographies, and plan programs. These library customers don't stay glued to your desk. Unfortunately, this cannot be said of the Clingers. With so much to do, it can be difficult to remain patient when a Clinger drops in for a long, long visit.

Clingers crave attention and monopolize time. They enjoy the social interaction with library staff, but always seem to overstay their welcome and consume enormous amounts of staff time. Some conduct actual library business, but then linger well beyond their transactions. Some are mentally challenged and don't understand that their clinginess becomes a nuisance. Others are simply seeking human contact. This is what makes Clingers such a challenge. They tend to be lonely people, and if you know their history, it makes it hard to tell them to stay away unless they have legitimate library business. Library staff is expected to be friendly and receptive to all customers, but there's also work to be done.

Clingers seem to think the librarian has nothing better to do than to chat with them. They don't recognize your personal space, and stand too close to you. In some cases, they even have to be shooed from behind the public desks.

Bob was our main Clinger. To make matters worse, he paid little or no attention to personal hygiene. A chain smoker with nails and teeth yellowed in testament to his constant habit, Bob reeked of smoke. Adding to that, his lack of cleanliness made his daily closeness hard to handle. Bob would hang around the reference desk, never taking the hint when we said we were busy. In fact, he didn't leave even when we were direct with him. He apparently figured he had a right to stay at the reference desk.

When other customers came up with reference questions, Bob would butt in with advice or "answers." When we'd remind Bob that a person's reference questions were personal, he'd step a few feet to the side. Unfortunately, as soon as we finished with that patron's request, Bob snapped back to the desk as though it was metal and he was a magnet. His behavior was perpetual, and so were our requests for him to leave the desk. Just about everyone on staff had spoken to Bob about his constant presence at the desk. Bob acted as though we were speaking about someone else. We tried the technique that had worked with most of our other Clingers: having a fellow staff member say to the person working at reference, "Mr. Griffiths needs you to phone him right away," giving the staff member a chance to escape from the desk and Bob's clutches; but it didn't work for Bob. He just waited patiently by the empty desk until the staff member returned. He never did anything bad enough for us to ask him to leave the library, although frankly, this would have helped us in the long run. Our experience with Bob taught us an important lesson: sometimes problems just don't go away, and you have to deal with them every time they come up.

It's important to remain courteous and professional with all customers, including those you may desperately want to avoid. Passing the Clinger off on another staff member isn't a solution. In fact, it may encourage the Clinger to stay longer, and start all over with a new listener. Instead, try ending the visit as tactfully as you can. As with all customers, be fair and consistent in your treatment of Clingers, and be straightforward about the reason you need to end the visit. Offer a polite apology and explain that you really need to get back to work. Then thank the Clinger for the visit and resume your duties. If leaving the public floor is an option, move to a restricted area where you can continue working undisturbed.

Obviously, not all library staff will have this luxury. You can also arrange for another staff member to ask to see you when the Clinger arrives. For those instances where staff has chronic problems with a Clinger and can't leave their posts, the library manager should step in and discourage that person from disrupting the staff. Another technique that works with some patrons is for the staff member to say to the Clinger, "I need to go to [someplace near the exit]. May I walk you to the door?" Regretfully, none of these remedies worked with Bob.

Most Clingers are harmless, overly friendly people who interrupt an otherwise productive day. For example, a very nice young man, probably 17 or 18 years of age, is a regular at one library's bookmobile stops. He comes for a visit each week, as much to talk as to pick up books. He likes to tell his life story, with all its trials and tribulations, including girl troubles. With this teen, it's hard for staff to maintain a professional distance and not get involved, no matter how much they remind themselves that they're not counselors, but they must.

As long as Clingers aren't threatening or disruptive, they have as much right as anyone to visit their public library and stay for as long as they like. However, that doesn't include monopolizing staff and creating such a nuisance that staff can't do their work. It's up to the library manager to determine how long is too long for Clingers and enforce that limit consistently.

Clingers who are new to your library should be regarded with a bit of skepticism, at least until you get to know their habits. Keep an eye on any staff or customer who becomes the target of an unfamiliar Clinger. Intervene if necessary. You never know when a Clinger could turn out to be a stalker.

The library manager is ultimately responsible for maintaining a safe environment for the employees and customers. Take control of excessive or inappropriate Clinger attention that keeps staff from their work or creates a hostile environment. Your employees will appreciate your support and your Clinger will learn the boundaries of your tolerance. Through it all, keep your cool and be professional, but firm. Remember to be direct. Clingers tend to not take hints.

If your Clinger encounter escalates into something potentially dangerous, or if your Clinger shows signs of stalking, for example, following staff members out to their cars, be prepared to take appropriate action. Use caution and, if necessary, call 911 for help. As is the case with other problem patrons, document both the Clinger's actions and yours, and, if you think it's necessary, contact local law enforcement; it's best to err on the side of caution.

In Summary

Clingers monopolize staff time and interfere with library business. Often, they are just lonely people who yearn for social contact, and will linger long after their transactions are completed. Some Clingers are mentally ill. Staff should remain courteous and professional to the Clingers and not pass them off to other staff. Tact is the best method of extricating yourself from the Clingers. If you see another staff member who has been cornered by a Clinger, walk over and see if you can assist. If everything else has failed, call the manager. If the Clinger appears to be dangerous and begins exhibiting stalker-like behavior, such as following staff outside the library, contact the police. (See Appendix B.)

DECEIVERS: LYING AS A WAY OF LIFE

> Oh what a tangled web we weave,
> When first we practise to deceive!
>
> —Sir Walter Scott

Have you ever noticed how easily some people lie? They look you right in the eye, and without missing a beat, relay a total falsehood. Your library probably has more than its share of Deceivers.

Even mothers lie. Our library had one such woman who would bring back a whole stack of picture books and claim that every one of them was marked by crayons when she checked them out. It struck us as odd that some juvenile defacer had checked out exactly the same titles she had, especially after this happened more than once. We put a note in her record and the third or fourth time, we charged her for damaged materials. In the case of crayoned books, it's important that the staff members who check in materials pay attention to the condition of the materials they're working with. Inattentive check-in staff pretty much destroys any case you have against people who destroy books and then lie about it. Staff needs to be taught to scrutinize the condition of returned materials before they check them in. The condition of the item as well as the precise type and location of damage(s) should be documented.

Deceivers might be people who have their original library card blocked because they owe lots of money or have lost materials, so they claim that they've never had a card before in an attempt to get a new one to borrow or steal more materials. When you pull up their existing record and ask, "Did you ever live at . . .?", of course, they deny it. Solution: Be prepared-Always cross check the birthdate.

You may have lots of John Smiths, but how many were born on the same date? Make sure your policies and procedures include always asking for a picture ID and proof of current address when issuing a new library card. Even if you have 20 "John Smiths," make sure staff is prepared to take the time to review each and every record to make sure that the present John is indeed a new person, not someone trying to escape an obligation. In the latest iteration of our circulation policy, we enter a patron's driver's license or state-issued ID number as their alternative ID number, since that probably never changes, and by finding the driver's license number in their record, we can be sure it's the same person.

One librarian commented, "If I had my way, we'd have a webcam at each circ station and we'd snap their picture whenever they apply for a library card. It would be in their record and appear on the monitor each time we pulled up the record. My eye doctor does this, so why can't the library?"

When you're dealing with Deceivers, also watch out for Schemers. These people actually plan their deception in advance. Sometimes, they're so good at lying that it makes you almost believe they're telling the truth, even if you know they aren't.

In Summary

Deceivers will tell you anything to get out of paying library fines or making compensation for lost or damaged materials. You will never catch all the Deceivers and schemers in your customer base, but you can discourage some of them by taking simple precautions, such as noticing the condition of materials before they're checked in or verifying that customers' IDs match their library records.

ENTITLED: JUST BECAUSE WE ARE

> There's no such thing as entitlement, unless someone has first met an obligation.
> —Margaret Thatcher, interview in *Women's Own* magazine, October 31, 1987

People feel entitled for a number of reasons. Some people feel entitled because of their income or wealth. Our library staff never really dealt with wealthy people until an area was developed on the north side of the city to attract affluent people. Eventually, the population grew to a point where a branch library was justified, and we became acquainted with the wealthy "Entitled." Granted, they were still only a small percentage of the neighborhood people using the library, but they were both vocal and tenacious.

Not all Entitled people are rich. Some people feel entitled because of the position they hold. Other people feel entitled because of the people they know.

The Entitled fall under the category "the I-have-a-right-to-be-rude customer." With their attitude that you're just a public servant, and it's your job to accept that premise as truth, it's hard not to react to them, especially when what you want to say is, "Didn't your mother teach you any manners?"

Mr. Smith is a "headache on purpose," who loves to give the staff a hard time. He simply refuses to carry his library card, saying, when we ask for it, "I don't make a habit of carrying it around." In a pinch, we allow registered patrons to check out items with a picture ID, but, of course, this is more difficult and time consuming for staff. Mr. Smith seems to have realized this and loves to create more work for staff. On one occasion, when a staff member who did not know him asked Mr. Smith to confirm his phone number for verification, Mr. Smith insolently replied, "I'm not in the habit of giving out my phone number." The staff member replied, "And I'm not in the habit of checking out items to people who are insolent." This wasn't the best response the staff member could have given, because it could have been done in a more polite, patient manner with the same result, but it did open a window for a staff member to speak to Mr. Smith about his attitude toward staff.

This same Mr. Smith had a habit of taunting one of our female staff members by asking her, "What are you doing behind that computer? Looking at porn?" Deeply offended, the staff member refused to wait on Mr. Smith and left the desk whenever he approached. We found it necessary to have the security guard stand behind a staff member whenever Mr. Smith was at the desk so he would behave. Eventually, the manager had a heart-to-heart talk with Mr. Smith, showing him our acceptable behavior policy (see Appendix C) and reminding him that if he was not polite to staff, he would be banned from the library. Incredibly, it worked, because Mr. Smith is an avid reader, and apparently, having access to books trumps his love of being obnoxious to the staff.

In Summary

You should have a section in your behavior policy to deal with rude and inappropriate behavior. Sometimes it takes a firm but polite hand in dealing with the Entitled. Be polite in dealing with the Entitled, and be sure to remind them that policies and rules apply to everyone across the board.

MONOPOLIZERS: IT'S ALWAYS *OUR* TURN

> Share everything.
> —Robert Fulghum, *All I Really Need to Know I Learned in Kindergarten*, 1986

Like all library assets, the electronic equipment provided for public access is a shared resource. (See Appendix D.) The equipment is maintained to prolong its useful life, and under normal conditions, it should last for many years. However, it should be supervised to ensure it is being handled as intended. The use of catalog terminals, Internet-access computers, gaming computers, and other electronic assets should be monitored to allow all patrons a reasonable opportunity to use them.

Waiting indefinitely for equipment to become available can, understandably, cause tempers to flare. Frustrated customers will either take matters into their own hands, or turn to their busy librarian to dispense justice. By taking a proactive approach to managing equipment usage, customers are forewarned of operator rules and time limitations. It won't eliminate the problem entirely, but a great majority of customers are cooperative and willing to abide by library policies.

Many libraries never seem to have enough catalog terminals and computer equipment to accommodate customers during peak demand hours, but by imposing time limitations or by assessing user fees, the equipment usage can be regulated for predefined periods of time.

Even with the cost of computer hardware becoming more affordable, it can be difficult to squeeze the cost of additional terminals into the budget. A number of national and local grant programs whose areas of interest include education and libraries are available. They are well worth the time to research and apply. But it's important to prepare for the ongoing costs of maintenance, software licensing, antivirus software, and even the eventual replacement of the equipment.

Coin-operated equipment, such as copy machines and printers, should be located in line-of-sight areas to discourage vandalism or theft. A well-stocked change machine located near the equipment will save time and keep customers from visiting the circulation desk for change. Some libraries have switched to prepaid debit cards to operate equipment.

The paper supply should also be monitored, both to keep the machine from running out of paper, and to keep the paper from running out the front door. We keep a bin with scratch paper in it on the desk. This way, people don't help themselves to fresh paper meant for printing when they only need to make notes. One word of caution about recycling paper for public use: be sure you don't recycle anything sensitive, such as personnel-related memos. These should be shredded.

The Monopolizer doesn't just refer to one-time equipment hogs. These people actually run their businesses from the library. One library had a patron conducting his eBay business on library equipment.

Some librarians have reported private tutors filling up the children's area every afternoon after school. These tutors use the library as a free, neutral place to tutor their students, for profit. Of course, study rooms might be available for a fee, but the tutors don't want to pay, even though they're making money tutoring at the library.

Not all business done at the library is on the up-and-up. When we saw the headlines one morning, no one was more surprised than we were that a fairly large prostitution ring had been operating in the small park in which our library is located. We knew about some of the illicit activities that went on there, such as the occasional drug deal, but we had no idea that as we quit for the evening, the ladies of the evening were just starting. About the same time we found out about the prostitution ring in the park, their illicit business came *inside* the library when johns began using our public phone to contact prostitutes they'd found online.

Nonprofit groups and clubs may want to monopolize display cases and bulletin boards. There are libraries where organizations have been so aggressive in monopolizing these resources, they have to be regulated. As a result, these librarians have had to limit the use of the display cases and bulletin boards to library-sponsored information and events. This is also true of meeting rooms. How many clubs and organizations can your library accommodate for their regular monthly meetings and still have facilities for library programs?

Monopolizers sometimes remind us of children hoarding their toys. They need to be dealt with directly. If they aren't, it's not fair to your other library customers. If the Monopolizers who aren't willing to share may need to be banned from the sandbox until they are.

In Summary

Some people just don't know how to play nice. They don't want to take turns using library equipment. They want only <u>their</u> information on library bulletin boards and in displays. They use library resources for profit-making endeavors. Libraries need policies in place about proper use of equipment and signage reminding people of these rules. Some also need to have specific policies for the use of bulletin boards, displays, and meeting rooms.

EXTREMISTS: PEOPLE WHO TAKE EVERYTHING TO THE OUTER LIMITS

Extremists think "communication" means agreeing with them.

—Leo Rosten

Many types of Extremists exist, and they are at both ends of every spectrum. Just to name a few, there are:

- Watchdog censors and people who believe that everything, even hate propaganda, should be in the library
- Pro-gun people and anti-gun people
- Big government supporters and anarchists
- Members of the far religious right and atheists
- Extreme pro-lifers and extreme pro-choicers

You get the picture. As polarized as their beliefs are, members of the extreme reaches of these groups share a distinguishing characteristic; they think the library should be solely *their* platform because theirs is the only true belief. They have the right to express their point of view, to the exclusion of all others.

One of our libraries was picked by the biggest pro-gun organization in the country as a test site for carrying guns in libraries. When we didn't comply with their demands, protests of armed people of all ages, including children, were staged near the library. Many of our customers refused to come to the library during these demonstrations. One protestor, a man with an assault weapon standing on a grassy knoll next to the building (the irony wasn't lost on us), waved his weapon in the direction of a patron who was entering the library. Words were exchanged, and pretty soon, there was a major fistfight by our front door.

The city attorney became involved with the talks between the library and the pro-gun group. Our state is renowned for its lax gun laws, and with this in mind, we began to negotiate. The protestors refused our suggestion to leave their guns in the trunks of their cars. They countered with an offer to check in their weapons with library staff until they were ready to leave the building. None of us wanted to handle or babysit a loaded weapon.

After much debate, we reached a compromise: The library would provide lockable metal cabinets in the archway just outside the front door where they could leave their weapons. This seemed to be agreeable to both parties, although neither side was completely happy with the solution. Despite our dwindling budget, we installed the expensive cabinets, and the protests and talks were over. Not one person used the cabinets. In fact, that was the last we saw of the protesters.

Religious organizations often donate materials to libraries. We try to represent as many as possible in our collection. However, some religious organizations want everything their church has ever published to be added to the library. In addition to this, they want materials featuring differing beliefs removed from the shelves.

A particular cult provided us with new copies of their books every year with no understanding of the costs involved in cataloging and processing them and expected us to make them available when they were hot off the press. We've also had problems with one religious group trying to monopolize all of our bulletin board space. When we asked another particularly zealous group not to proselytize in the library, they quit approaching our other patrons; but they hid their pamphlets inside library books and magazines.

At some point, an organization of atheists noticed that we had books on a lot of religions. They protested our having any materials at all from religious groups because it went against what they felt was the concept of the division of church and state. We ended up compromising by accepting a gift subscription of their organization's magazine, and making sure we had plenty of books on atheism, too.

One library had a display case in the main foyer that could be reserved for a month at a time by members of the public to display their personal collections of dolls, stamps, butterflies, and others.

Although the area was available to the general public, the library wasn't overwhelmed with requests to display items; sometimes the case sat empty for weeks. That is, until a particular religious group began reserving the case for several months in a row. Though the displays were varied and interesting, and often, not of a particularly religious nature, library staff began to get questions from the public as to why this group was monopolizing the display case month after month. Because the library had no policy that stated otherwise, staff couldn't tell this group they had to take turns with the display area "just because." And passing a new policy limiting usage would seem like it was aimed specifically at them. Eventually, we developed a policy that limited the display case to one month a year, and during the months that weren't booked, we used the case to highlight new books.

Some extremist groups will even threaten you and your library. When Planned Parenthood offered to do free programs at our library for parents and 'tweens on what happens to your body as you grow up, there was so much interest that we had to do several sessions. A local pro-life organization took exception. They made threats against the library, threatened to disrupt the Planned Parenthood programs, and sent ominous letters to the branch managers saying they were the "spawns of Satan." They also sent them full-colored posters of aborted babies. We went ahead and held the instructional sessions with the 'tweens and their parents, and fortunately, despite the veiled and unveiled threats, nothing else happened.

Sometimes, extreme political groups will try to use your library for their own political purposes. They want to use your meeting rooms for their regular meetings. They want to present programs supporting their position. They want to post their propaganda on your bulletin board; and they want their petitions signed at your library.

In the park where one library is located, we've often had petitioners who've asked people for their signatures to nominate candidates, recall candidates, change bills, add bills, support causes, and so on. Some of the petitioners have been extraordinarily aggressive. They actually step in front of our patrons and almost demand that they sign their document. This prompted patrons to insist that our staff do something about it. We found that there was a limit mandated by law as to how close the petitioners could get to the library, and we enforced it. We also discovered that if we spoke calmly with the petitioners about their behavior, they usually respected our requests.

The rule has some exceptions. Recently, library staff had to break up opposing petitioners who were yelling at each other outside the library. Each one cited, loudly, his own version of the "first come, first served" rule. One staff member said, "This is city property. If you don't stop fighting, I'll call the police, and you both go." They stopped.

Be proactive in solving issues with Extremists. Have policies and procedures in place that establish the library as a place to be shared by all. These policies should cover collection development especially the policy on gifts and additions, as well as the use of materials, library space, and special areas, such as display cases and bulletin boards. Libraries should also have a worst-case policy and procedure in case things should escalate to demonstrations (see Appendix E).

Good, calm communication is the best way to deal with the Extremists. Never argue with them about their views. It's like author Robert Heinlein observed: "Never try to teach a pig to sing; it wastes your time and it annoys the pig."

In Summary

Every community has its share of Extremists. Dealing with Extremists is one area where your policies and rules have to be rock-solid. Make sure administration and the legal department approve your policies, and keep them in the loop when an extremist group has targeted your library to make a statement. When you deal with Extremists, keep calm and professional because their zeal can cause situations to go from bad to worse faster than you can say, "Are you a registered voter?

HARMLESS ECCENTRICS: LOCAL COLOR

That so few now dare to be eccentric marks the chief danger of the time.

—John Stuart Mill

It was our first ever multiday event at the library. Speakers and programs on solar energy were scheduled for the entire week. A large crowd had gathered in front of the library in anticipation of the first presentation and free treats. The vice mayor was giving the opening speech, and there was someone to translate what he'd said into Spanish.

Suddenly, his words were drowned out by the sound of a very loud honking noise, when, from around the corner of the building rode "Rooster." "Rooster," as he was known, was an eccentric person who practically lived on his bicycle. He never talked, but he loved to circle people, honking his horn as fast as he could. On this particular day, the person chosen for Rooster's attention was the vice mayor. Rooster circled around the podium several times. The vice mayor just smiled at him and waited patiently until Rooster honked his horn and drove away. Rooster and his routine only disrupted the proceedings for a short time; and frankly, his actions had entertainment value.

Probably some people at the opening event didn't know Rooster and wondered why someone hadn't called the police to take him away; but we knew that Rooster was one of our Harmless Eccentrics. Though he never talked, with his long, flyaway hair, large, staring eyes, and determined expression, every day he added color and interest to our library park.

Danny, who'd lived in our town most of his life, fried his brains with drugs during the 1960s. His mother went to San Francisco to bring him home, and shortly after this, Danny decided our library was his second home. It still is. For many years, Danny has come to the library every day it's open, rain or shine. He sits on a bench inside the archway beside the front entrance and plays his battered guitar. He only knows two or three chords, and never sings more than a brief phrase of the song he's selected, but he sings with enthusiasm and smiles brightly as each library customer walks to the door. On the rare occasion that Danny's not there, staff is asked by patrons where he is and if he's sick. Danny knows most of the staff by name, and calls the others by names he's made up for them. Danny is as much a part of the library and the park as the bronze statue of the old man feeding the pigeons.

John is a tuba player. For years, in the late afternoon, he sits on a park bench near the walkway to the library and plays songs, familiar and unfamiliar. He begins lots of melodies, but he only finishes a few. John even takes requests. He takes the stage about the same time Danny leaves. John doesn't come every day, but he's there often enough to be considered a regular part of life in our downtown community.

All sorts of people are drawn to libraries. The Harmless Eccentrics are some of the more interesting ones. Staff and patrons learn to coexist with them, and many enjoy their company. However, don't assume that strangers with odd behaviors are Harmless Eccentrics; they just might be dangerous.

In Summary

Harmless Eccentrics who have been in the community for years are part of the local color. They are well-known to staff and customers. Strangers who exhibit odd behaviors may be dangerous, and should not be categorized as Harmless Eccentrics.

SMELLY PEOPLE: THE HYGIENE DEFICIENT AND OTHER STINKY PATRONS

Man is a museum of diseases, a home of impurities; he comes today and is gone tomorrow; he begins as dirt and departs as stench.

—Mark Twain

A public library's customers are as diverse as its collection. A healthy mixture of cultures and age groups gives the facility its broad appeal; but let's face it: the world is a smelly place. Many cultures, particularly Western, are highly conscious of body odor, while people from other parts of the world aren't nearly so concerned. From a librarian's perspective, the old commercial slogan "Never let them see you sweat" isn't entirely accurate. Add to that the aftereffects of food choices and ineffective oral hygiene. There are those who smoke. There are those who enjoy a little garlic or onion with every meal. Others eat a lot of beans, bran, or prunes, if you get our drift.

Also some medical conditions cause halitosis. Sometimes, medications and various medical conditions create unpleasant body odors. Likewise, there are incontinent people and those who can't control their body functions. Whether by culture, circumstance, medical condition, or grooming, your library is a Petri dish of odors.

Personal grooming and hygiene habits are highly individual and not something we talk about in polite society. Simply agree to disagree. Accept the fact that some folks wash up every day but reserve bathing for Saturday nights, and they see no problem with getting an extra day or two of wear out of each outfit before laundering. Others can't start the day without a good, bracing shower and a fresh set of clothes. Few, if any, other countries are as obsessed by deodorant as the United States. Children bring their own special funk to the party, something they'll hopefully outgrow in puberty. So when these individuals converge at your library, along with their interesting fragrances, celebrate that diversity and remember the fact these are the people who use and support your library.

Babies are notorious odor makers. If your library doesn't already have diaper-changing stations in the restrooms, consider budgeting for them. Moms and dads alike will appreciate the courtesy. Designated changing stations will afford you the ability to restrict diaper changing from other areas of the library, like on the carpet or (ugh) the tables. If you have changing stations, remember to check them from time to time, and to keep them clean and sanitary throughout the day. A quick swipe with a disinfectant wipe will usually do the trick.

A quick side note. Some nursing mothers may choose to breastfeed during their visit to the library. Unless your state prohibits or restricts this activity, a mother is perfectly within her rights to nurse her baby in a public place. Become familiar with your state's laws regarding this practice in case you're challenged by other customers. Be prepared to react as appropriate. If need be, offer the nursing mom a quiet place where she can finish feeding her baby in private.

This brings us to the other smelly thing babies do: spit up. A sour-smelling baby is unpleasant for everyone, including the parent, particularly if the parent is the one wearing the curdle corsage. The customer's comfort is part of a librarian's job, and a little kindness and goodwill is not only courteous, it's good for business. Remember those disinfectant wipes from the changing station? Or those tissues in the desk drawer? Or how about a damp towel from the break room? Don't hesitate to offer something to help the parent with cleanup. It's these little courtesies that show customers they're valued and you get to clear the air at the same time.

In the confines of a public library, heavy perfume or excessive cologne can be as offensive as body odor. Like the earlier hygiene discussion, this grooming choice is up to the individual. The wearer doesn't mean to offend. In fact, it's entirely possible the wearers don't even realize how strongly they smell. For most customers, this may be a minor annoyance, but for others, like migraine sufferers or asthmatics, heavy concentrations of perfume or cologne can lead to medical issues. Keeping the library well ventilated will help soften the blow and freshen the air.

Be mindful that a person's smell or appearance isn't necessarily theirs by choice. Not everyone has personal transportation to drive to the library in air-conditioned comfort. A long bicycle ride or an extended wait at a hot bus stop can leave a person damp and funky. Others stop by the library after work, bearing the scent of an honest day's labor. None of these customers arrives as clean and fresh as the morning mist, but their visit to the library is obviously important to them and to you.

A few extreme customers may have body odor that goes beyond unpleasant to nauseating. They smell so bad that staff members literally do not want to wait on them. When they see one of these customers approaching the desk, they may intentionally delay by taking longer with their current customer, so someone else gets stuck with the person who stinks. Everyone deserves good customer service, including people who don't smell good.

Some libraries add a "Stinky Patron" or offensive odor rule to their codes of conduct. These are usually aimed at the homeless, but written so ambiguously that they could apply to just about anyone, and their enforcement, or lack thereof, lies in the sensibilities of the librarian on desk. Library rules should be objective, fair, easily defended, and uniformly enforced.

As we are not lawyers, this paragraph constitutes legal *information*, not legal *advice*. In 1992, Richard Kreimer, a homeless man in Morristown, New Jersey, sued the Joint Free Public Library of Morristown and Morris Township over a library policy banning people with an offensive odor. The lower court ruled in favor of Mr. Kreimer, but the U.S. Court of Appeals for the Third Circuit later upheld the validity of the library policy to limit access to the library. The case was a complicated one and libraries are urged to research the case and its outcomes before drafting a similar policy of their own.

Libraries are magnets for the homeless, who use the facility for shelter, restroom access and a clean, safe, quiet place to sleep. While homelessness is a terrible thing, the library is not equipped or intended to be a place to sleep. Know what local organizations have a specific mission of helping the homeless, and ask for their assistance with your library's transient residents (Appendix F). From time to time, our library is visited by a homeless person who just wants help finding a place to shower. It is harder than you can imagine to find a place where a person can clean up. Those may use the library's restrooms to wash, but once again, this is inadequate. We distribute a flyer at our library that lists resources for emergency housing, medical care, food, and others.

Sometimes a customer's poor hygiene habits will affect how they treat library materials. In one instance, a rather unkempt customer came to the circulation desk to return three VHS tapes and a DVD, which had been declared lost. As soon as staff opened the cassette cases to verify that the correct titles were inside, dozens of tiny cockroaches scrambled everywhere! We grabbed some plastic bags and double-bagged the items, which were hastily deposited into the dumpster behind the building. The library billed the customer for replacement videos, since the others were no longer suitable to circulate. A note was entered into the customer's record, warning staff to use caution with items returned by this customer. In addition, the customer was advised on how to properly store and care for library materials in her home. Remember, your library's reputation is at stake with every item you lend.

Never assume your that library is immune from pest invasions. Even our nation's iconic Library of Congress had a lice epidemic. Stay alert for infestations.

In Summary

Every person who walks into your library has the potential to make it a stinkier place. Babies, people with certain medical conditions, smokers, manual laborers who come straight to the library after work, even people who wear too much perfume, cologne, or aftershave. Homeless people, who are offered few opportunities to shower, often have a strong body odor. There are cultures where, unlike American society, body odor isn't such a big thing. Keep your library well ventilated, and learn not to judge people by how they smell.

KNOW-IT-ALLS: PEOPLE WHO DON'T NEED A REFERENCE LIBRARIAN

He that speaks much, is much mistaken.

—Benjamin Franklin

Do you think Benjamin Franklin had problem patrons in the Library Company of Philadelphia? We bet he did, unless basic human nature was different in 1731, and our guess is that his problem patrons included Know-It-Alls. Librarians today have centuries of history and fancy college degrees that make us authorities on library management. Poor old Ben had to wing it.

We can just hear the town Know-It-All:

- "A due date? Why can I not keep my books for as long as I wish? 'Twould be more charitable."
- "Why dost thou have so many books about sharpening plow shears? If thee ask me, there should be more books about butter churning. That's what thy people desire."
- "Electricity in lightning bolts? That can't be right. Thee and thy darned fool notions."

Poor Ben indeed. With all of his brilliance, even he was probably no match for the Colonial Know-It-All.

We can always count on Know-it-Alls for their probing questions. Of course, their wealth of knowledge doesn't stop here. Oh heavens, no. They also know better ways to set and enforce library policies, which items to add or remove from the collection, how to completely overhaul the checkout process, and which of the library staff needs to be fired.

Ben would be the first to admit that you can't please all of the people all of the time. This is especially true of the Know-It-Alls. They tend to have strong opinions on just about everything. Take collection development: contrary to what some folks think, acquisition decisions aren't made using a blindfold and a dartboard. Librarians who know their communities and understand their circulation patterns base their collection development on real data. This is particularly true in this era of library automation. Old Ben would appreciate the irony.

Librarians know, even in flush economic times, that managing the core collection, renewing subscriptions, updating reference materials, and purchasing new self-help and bestsellers can be daunting. When the budget is tight it's even more difficult, particularly while the collection is aging with no means to replace it. If the library carries popular movies or gaming software, the purchasing decisions become even harder as these items compete for the already limited funding. Of course, your Know-It-Alls tell you exactly what should have been purchased, and where you failed. In short, they would have done a better job.

Usually, Know-It-Alls critique the collection without seeing the big picture, like a book budget that's been cut, or the rising cost of materials. They may not consider that not everyone comes to the library for the same reason they did.

The book collection is a library staple, but movies and games are popular with many customers too, who use the library as a source of free entertainment. There's nothing wrong with that. Some customers come in just to use the computers. Why not? That's what they are there for.

Our library had one Know-It-All in particular who not only ran a constant commentary on what books we should buy, but also where to buy them. He would check with his preferred bookstore to see if we had shopped there, and yelled at us because we never did. A big part of this was because of the purchasing regulations that dictated how we order materials. He let everyone know that buying DVDs, CDs, and games was a waste of public funds, and that since the word "library" comes from the word for book, that's what we should focus on. If you've done your diligence to get the most from your acquisitions budget, there is nothing to apologize for. Simply accept the Know-It-All's criticism as a suggestion and move on to the next, hopefully more pleasant, customer.

We've had Know-It-Alls offer their wisdom at the reference desk while we are assisting other customers. The reference staff provides fact-based information, from well-established resources. The Know-It-Alls may be knowledgeable, but like Wikipedia, they're not always the ideal sources for correct answers. Be sure your reference customers receive the right information, and save your debate with the Know-It-All for some other time. Be warned; whatever right answer you may give them, they will always have one that's righter.

Library policies are another popular Know-It-All target. Prepare to be challenged. The amount of time and thought invested in solid policies, with roots dating back to Colonial times, doesn't matter to the Know-It-All. Library policies exist for your protection and for the orderly operation of your library, and they are your shield against the Know-It-All's objections. If everyone complains, maybe the policy needs to change. If only the Know-It-Alls complain, your policy is probably working just fine.

A great deal of social debate covers what makes Know-It-Alls behave the way they do. We find it interesting that, according to Mayoclinic.com, many Know-It-All behaviors are similar to those associated with certain personality disorders: extreme perfectionism, an obsession with rules, and a need to control the order of things. It poses an interesting possibility. But then, we're librarians, not psychologists. There are all sorts of reasons for Know-It-Alls to act as they do. The important thing is deciding how to respond to them.

Dealing effectively with Know-It-All customers is all about patience. Listening to their suggestions costs you nothing but a bit of your time. Even if their "better" way to do things is never used, you've given it your consideration. If they question you about their suggestion when it fails to materialize, be prepared to explain why. Of course, they will believe you are wrong.

Unwarranted complaints against the library staff should not be tolerated. Some Know-It-Alls accelerate to bullying techniques in attempting to intimidate staff, and then lodge a complaint when staff doesn't comply with their demands. Your employees should be confident in enforcing library policies, knowing management has their backs.

Except for a possible blow to the ego, there's nothing to fear from the Know-It-All's behavior. They can be stubborn, intrusive, and very opinionated, but they rarely act out in anger. They're mainly annoyed by what they perceive as the ineptitude of everyone else; but beware. The Know-It-All is at his most annoying when he's right and you're wrong!

In Summary

Know-It-Alls can do everything better than you can. They know which books you should have purchased, what services you should offer, how you should answer reference questions, and even where you should buy library materials. The best way to interact with the Know-It-All is to be patient, listen quietly, and not argue. Don't take their criticisms personally. After all, they really don't know it all!

LOUD CUSTOMERS: PEOPLE WHO NEED A VOLUME CONTROL KNOB

Here is where people,
One frequently finds,
Lower their voices
And raise their minds.

—Richard Armour, "Library"

The Hollywood image of the angry, pinched-faced librarian with her index finger pressed sternly to her lips is a stereotype most of us librarians detest. We don't peer over the reference desk like hawks on the hunt, or bob up like curious prairie dogs every time someone whispers in the stacks. Seriously, where do they get this stuff?

Actually, over the years librarians have become more tolerant to noise than they once were. Copy machines, printers, and even quiet conversations are the new white noise of the library. These are perfectly acceptable. Disruptive sounds, the ones that disturb the peacefulness for other library customers, are another matter. Raised voices, outbursts of laughter, loud music, rambunctious children, and other distracting sounds fall into this category. If the noise is disturbing you, it's probably bothering your customers, too, even if no one complains. It's up to you to take the initiative and restore order. Don't make your customers come to you.

Disruptive behavior can include loud music or singing, too. Recently, a Whistler began coming to the library. He comes in almost every day with his hat and overcoat on, even in warm weather and just seems to wander around the library distractedly. He often whistles while he wanders. He complies when we ask him not to whistle in the library, but with his next visit, the whistling begins again.

Libraries are social gathering places intended as much for entertainment as learning. We face a challenge every day, to encourage the social use, which tends to be noisy, while protecting the scholarly use, which prefers a quiet environment. Library design, furnishings, and layout can eliminate a lot of the noise, but sometimes it's necessary for staff to become the enforcers.

In libraries large enough to provide the space, the children's department is in an entirely separate area where children can read, play, and just be children. However, rowdy children who escape into the adult area can be problematic. When it comes to children, an increase in physical activity is usually in direct proportion to an increase in loudness. For example, a child who is running through the library is probably also laughing and being chased by another child who is either shouting or crying. Sounds familiar? Before you know it, the one or two overstimulated children escalate into even more kids running and yelling through the library. It's as contagious as measles and must be stopped before it spreads.

One approach, if they're old enough to respond to reason, is to ask them politely to be quiet. However, don't be unrealistic and expect silence from children, just a lower noise level will suffice. You can explain to them that people are studying in the library, and it's difficult to concentrate or learn with so much noise going on. Invite them to return to the children's department, where they might find something more interesting and constructive to do. If you're lucky, this will calm them down, at least for a while. If you're not, and the behavior continues, they'll need to leave the library until they can be quieter.

Of course, this is only an option for older, independent children who are capable of being out on their own. For younger children, their parents should be somewhere in the library. Locate them and enlist their help in controlling their children. If the parents can't be located, there are larger issues to consider, now that you are essentially responsible for someone else's unsupervised child. The "Kid Dumpers" section offers information on how to manage this situation.

Some libraries have areas designed specifically for teens, where they can socialize without disturbing other customers. The books and magazines in this area are targeted to the interests of this age group, so teens are drawn into it naturally and tend to stay there to socialize. However, this area must also have a noise limit for when the fun gets out of hand. The number of warnings you allow before asking the offenders to leave is up to you, but we recommend your first warning be your only warning. Repeated warnings weaken your authority and will become a game you will never win. Remain professional and respectful, but be direct and when challenged, follow through. It's important that the library have a policy to cover these situations describing the number of warnings allowable and the follow-up consequences, such as banning.

People who are hearing-impaired often use louder voices without even realizing it. What's more, they may not be able to hear you unless you use a louder voice too. Under the circumstances, if increased volume is needed to conduct business with these customers, reasonable people will understand the loud conversation is necessary and only temporary. Keep your conversation succinct and to the point, ending it as soon as possible for the sake of other patrons.

Some people are louder because of cultural differences. To an outsider, their conversations seem high-volume, and agitated, accompanied with a plethora of hand and arm gestures. Usually, if you just walk over and greet them in a low voice, they get the hint.

We all know people who have naturally loud voices. Even their whispers resonate. For these customers, try speaking more softly, which may prompt them to do the same. Like the hearing-impaired customers, loud talkers may not be presently aware they're exceeding the library's acceptable decibel limit. Many of them realize their booming voices carry; they just need to be reminded of it, and are willing to lower the volume.

Perhaps the most difficult of the Loud Customers are the human bulldozers who use volume to get their way. These customers also fit the bully profile, the in-your-face customers who revel in taking advantage of others. They're more than loud. They're rude. Some interrupt. Some even push through to the head of the line.

Don't encourage them by allowing this behavior to go unchallenged. Point out to line-crashers that the person behind them was next, and invite the bulldozers to quietly wait their turn. Some bulldozers will comply but others will object, loudly, maybe even cause scenes as bullies so often do. Whatever the outburst, you must do what's fair for everyone and ignore the bulldozer's theatrics. If the disgruntled bulldozer storms off and never comes back, the library is a quieter place for it.

Other potentially disruptive noisemakers are loud ringtones and customers taking calls in the library. We're not unreasonable people. We can tolerate quick exchanges that end before they create problems. It's the longer, louder conversations, even arguments that need to be taken outside. For greater leverage in controlling cell phone use, try posting signs at the entrances prohibiting customers from making and taking cell phone calls inside the library.

Some states have laws against making noise in the library. For example, it's a crime to be noisy in a Massachusetts library:

Part IV Crimes, Punishments and Proceedings in Criminal Cases
Title I Crimes and Punishments

Chapter 272 Crimes Against Chastity, Morality, Decency and Good Order

§ 41. Disturbance—Public Libraries.

Whoever willfully disturbs persons assembled in a public library, or a reading room connected therewith, by making a noise or in any other manner during the time when such library or reading room is open to the public shall be punished as provided in the preceding section.

Life is noisy, and sometimes people need to be reminded of library etiquette. It doesn't take a pinched face or an angry *shush*, just a little patience and consistency.

In Summary

It's unrealistic to expect complete silence in your library. However, noise that is disruptive to customers should be discouraged. Rambunctious, unruly children in the adult area should be instructed to return to the children's department. Boisterous teens are welcome to socialize quietly but loud behavior needs to be discouraged. You need to recognize why your customers are being loud. Be tactful with the hearing impaired, who may not realize how loud they are; sometimes they can't help using an unusually loud speaking voice. For those who come from cultures where speech is more animated or for those people who are naturally loud, you might try speaking more softly, thus encouraging them to follow suit. Intentionally Loud Customers who use volume to bully others should not be allowed to take advantage or receive preferential treatment. You might have to resort to using your library's behavior policy. The use of cell phones should be regulated or discouraged. Some silence is still golden.

SHY, QUIET MUMBLERS: WHAT WAS THAT AGAIN?

> Nine-tenths of the serious controversies in life result from misunderstanding.
>
> —Louis Brandeis

Some Mumblers don't want to raise their voice in the library. Sometimes they're people who are chewing gum. Sometimes they've had dental work or a recently pierced tongue. However, Mumblers are usually those shy, quiet customers who speak so softly it's difficult to hear or understand what they want. They prefer to remain at the fringes, patiently waiting to be acknowledged rather than stepping forward and asking for help.

These customers are perfectly lovely people who sometimes need a little coaxing to get them to speak up. For example, the Mumbler will approach the reference desk but wait a few paces back, reluctant to interfere with the busy librarian's work, even though that work consists of assisting customers at the desk, including the Mumbler. It's an interesting paradox. In many cases, Mumblers will allow other customers to step up to the desk ahead of them, content to let others cut in ahead while they continue to wait patiently for the librarian to acknowledge them.

One of our Mumblers doesn't like to talk to men. She refuses to use the self-check, so she'll hover around in view of the circulation desk until a woman comes on duty; then, she'll check out her items.

It's important for staff to be aware of the customers around the desk, particularly the customers who've been there a while, like the Mumblers who find it difficult to assert themselves. A cheerful, "May I help you find something?" is often enough of an invitation to get Mumblers to open up. Be patient and prepared to listen carefully because in addition to being shy, they're also very quiet.

In order to ensure you understand their request correctly, it helps to ask them to write down the name of the author or title they're looking for. If they have a reference question, ask for clarification on any part of their request you didn't hear clearly. And proceed at their pace, even if it means the next customer has to wait a little longer. Don't frustrate or embarrass the Mumblers by rushing and pushing them beyond their social comfort zone. Just speaking to you may be more difficult for them than you realize.

At the circulation desk, where customers usually wait in a more organized line, Mumblers don't have to compete for a chance to approach the desk. However, once they arrive at checkout, their shy, quiet ways may make it difficult to communicate. Staff should be trained to treat all customers with respect, even the ones that require a little extra effort.

In Summary

Shy, quiet Mumblers find it difficult to ask for assistance and tend to speak quietly. If you have trouble hearing them or miss any part of their question, diplomatically ask them to write it down so they receive correct information. Use patience and that little bit of extra effort to make sure your communication is accurate.

POLITICAL CAMPAIGNERS: PERPETUAL PETITIONERS

> I do not believe that any political campaign justifies the declaration of a moratorium on ordinary common sense.
>
> —Dwight D. Eisenhower

In recent years, it seems as though we're always in the middle of one political campaign or another. No sooner does one end when another begins. And if your community is like ours, there is no shortage of political issues or candidates.

Because libraries attract such a diverse cross-section of the population, they're convenient locations for Campaigners to encounter large numbers of potential voters and gain support for their political platforms. By greeting the library customers approaching the entrance, candidates gain valuable face time that political advertising just can't buy. It isn't only candidates who use the library for their publicity forum. Citizens gathering signatures for ballot petitions often set up shop outside the entrance to solicit support from approaching customers.

All of this politicking can become a hassle for your customers, especially those who have already decided how they're going to vote in the upcoming election, or those who support the other candidate. Most of them just want to get inside and go about their business. Fortunately, in our experience, candidates and petition workers tend to be reasonable people. They don't want to create conflict and negative publicity by being pushy or rude. Still, even the most nonthreatening political activity should be managed to keep it from becoming a nuisance.

Campaign flyers are not usually permitted inside libraries. The library is not a campaign headquarters. Besides that, there could be candidates running against your current mayor or city council, which could easily be a political nightmare. The Hatch Act, which is explained on the U.S. Office of Special Counsel website, gives specifics on what limitations a government employee has when it comes to campaigning.

Like it or not, libraries can be important components of campaign strategies. Not only are they ideal for meet-and-greet opportunities, they're often also voter registration sites. Candidates can gain supporters outside the library, and then encourage them to register to vote when they get inside. That's pretty smart when you think about it. We provide the audience and the venue, and then create new, card-carrying voters to boot.

The library too can benefit from all of these political glad-handers posted literally at the doorstep. Campaigners can become powerful allies, particularly candidates for local office. If they're elected, these people will probably be making your funding decisions. It pays to have a strong advocate or two at the bargaining table. Cultivate these positive relationships early and make your concerns known.

Of course, there are some Campaigners who just don't get it. Their behavior may come across as overly aggressive or even offensive to your customers. While most signature gatherers seem enthusiastic about their ballot initiatives, a few go too far and become pushy or even argumentative. We've even had to call the police about some of them. When the political activity outside leads to customer complaints inside, it means it is time for library management to get involved. No candidate or cause is worth losing your customers when there are plenty of other places the Campaigners can go to conduct their business.

In Summary

Libraries are popular places for politicians and ballot initiative supporters to campaign. Outside politicking should not extend into the library. These candidates can be powerful allies. Campaigners who become aggressive or argumentative should be invited to leave.

RELIGIOUS PROSELYTIZERS: THE LIBRARY IS THEIR MISSION FIELD

> Religion is like a pair of shoes. Find one that fits for you, but don't make me wear your shoes.
> —George Carlin

Few places symbolize America's freedom of speech and expression like modern libraries. Customers are free to enjoy the collection, the exhibits, and the programs to whatever extent they want, or they can simply browse for a while and walk away with no pressure, no questions, no obligation. This personal liberty is part of the library's appeal. It's very important to protect it, particularly from people who use the opportunity to take advantage of your library traffic to convert your customers to their belief systems. Libraries are favorite fishing holes for Religious Proselytizers who want to impose their beliefs on the steady stream of customers visiting the library. While these public preachers may feel their actions are justified, their presence is often an unwelcome intrusion, much like political campaigners and panhandlers. It may seem harmless to allow this activity, but permitting one religion to do it invites all others to cast their nets on your customers, too.

Some Proselytizers limit their contact to simply passing out religious literature and offering friendly smiles. Customers need barely break stride as they pass by and either accept or decline the offered materials. This passive approach is less intrusive, but your customers may still complain. People don't tend to visit their library to find salvation. The other fallout from the brochure distributors is those pamphlets accepted outside tend to be promptly discarded all over the place inside.

The library manager or the collection development supervisor is generally responsible for what's in the collection. Any items made available to the customers should have the manager's approval. Unless those accumulated religious flyers left behind by Proselytizers are part of your library's collection strategy, they should be removed as soon as they're discovered. Items allowed to remain on display encourage Proselytizers to leave more, and before long, it becomes an expectation.

Some may take a more assertive approach, and with missionary zeal, might even physically confront your library customers, blocking their entrance to the library. Dealing with the nuisance Proselytizers should be done with kindness. Most are perfectly lovely people who believe in what they're doing. Your job is merely to encourage them to do it somewhere else. Even moving them a short distance away from the entrance can make all the difference in the world. In our experience, most Proselytizers are cooperative and happy to comply. You might also mention that your collection contains a variety of spiritual and inspirational titles for interested customers, and offer to have a book in the collection representing their religion. However, there are still those who feel it is their duty to dispense religion at the library door.

Of course, not all religious missioners are peaceful. Some zealots take a hard-line approach, preaching a message of vengeance and damnation, and loudly. Any effort to discourage them from harassing people feeds directly into their rhetoric of fear. Those who confront them are heretics for interfering with God's will, which apparently includes harassing library customers.

When dealing with the zealots, it's imperative to remain calm and professional. Engaging in a shrieking contest won't solve anything. However, any zealots worth their salt won't let a little obstacle like library policy stop them. If the obnoxious behavior gets out of hand, it may be necessary to contact security or the local police and report the nuisance to them. While there is probably nothing illegal about what they're doing, their ranting does interfere with library business.

Zealots can potentially create a hostile environment that could result in an altercation, injury or damage. For example, we had a street preacher yell at one of our regular customers as he walked toward the library, "You're going to Hell!" The library customer didn't take kindly to his pronouncement, and promptly punched the other guy in the nose. Even in noncombative situations, the customers and your staff quickly tire of being hassled every time they come to the library.

Some angry Proselytizers may actually be dangerous, either mentally or emotionally unstable. (See Appendix B.) If you sense a reason for concern, approach them with caution and bring another person or two, preferably police or security. Prepare your staff for situations that could become volatile. Discourage heroics and leave the dangerous work to the professionals.

Your library policy prohibiting proselytizing on the premises should be enforced uniformly and tactfully. The language should be broad enough to encompass all forms of religious or cult sermonizing directed at library customers and staff. It should also prohibit leaving religious flyers and booklets in the library. You may soften the policy to allow items such as announcements of concerts or cultural events at religious institutions such as a Greek Fest at the local Greek Orthodox Church or a choral performance of *The Messiah* at a nearby Methodist Church to be posted on the public bulletin board, one to a customer, and only for a specified period of time. Check the board regularly to ensure it isn't being monopolized, and clear it often, perhaps weekly. That way, customers have access to the information if they want it, or they can simply browse for a while and walk away, no pressure, no questions, no obligation.

In Summary

Public gathering places, such as libraries, are prime recruitment places for Religious Proselytizers. Unfortunately, library customers often find this sharing of faith, however well intended, to be an uncomfortable, unwanted intrusion. Preaching that becomes overly aggressive should be discouraged. There is nothing wrong with proselytizing, as long as it doesn't interfere with library business or your customers' entrance into the library.

SLOBS: MESSY EATERS, CHEWING GUM ARCHIVISTS, AND OTHER UNTIDY PEOPLE

> Human beings are flawed and complicated and messy.
>
> —Brit Marling

Anyone who's had their foot stuck to the floor of a movie theater knows that people can be Slobs. Part of this is a basic lack of respect for others' property. Part of it may be the result of a lifetime of laziness and slovenly habits. At some point, the Slob's bad behavior will impact your library.

A few years ago, we were renovating our library. Our leaky roof ended up taking the lion's share of our funds, so we decided to spruce up our existing furniture instead of buying new. When we turned over our tables to work on the legs, we discovered a mosaic of chewing gum under each one. Some of the gum clumps were ancient and petrified. Some were still soft. One of our staff members, to whom we are forever grateful, volunteered to scrape the gum from the underside of every chair and table in the building. It took hours to finish the job. Our guess is that, unless you're diligent about removing it, there's probably a goodly supply of gum under your tables, too.

Slobs leave their scraps of paper on the floor or wad them up and leave them by the computers. They sneak in food and leave the greasy wrappings and remains for you to clean up. They spill things on your books, smear their food on your furniture, and leave their bottles and Styrofoam cups right where they finished their drinks.

Sandwich wrappers, empty drink containers, and even leftovers have no place in the library. Many libraries prohibit customers from bringing food or beverages into the facility. This is one of the surest ways to prevent damage to books, furniture, and equipment.

Unfortunately, no matter how many rules you make, how well you clean up, or how many garbage cans you set around your facility, the Slobs will find a way to mess it up. We found that by asking <u>every</u> staff member and volunteer to be on the lookout for trash in the library, we were able to keep on top of the daily messes. We also had a "Clean Team" that did a thorough inspection of the library once a month, or more frequently, if needed. The Clean Team also reported such things as burned-out light bulbs, loose drawer handles, and graffiti.

A full-time, or even a half-time, custodian assigned specifically to the library is getting to be a luxury, a thing of the past. Many libraries are at the mercy of part-time and usually low bid contract cleaners. You know that nebulous phrase, ". . . and other jobs as assigned by the supervisor." A clean library is a public expectation. Part of your job, no matter what your title, should be to help keep it that way.

In Summary

It seems as though Slobs are ubiquitous. They have no respect for the property of others, and think nothing of littering your library with their trash. Your entire staff, as well as your volunteers, need to be on the lookout for messes left by the Slobs, and take responsibility for properly disposing of their cups, food remains, wrappers, bottles, and other junk. It isn't fair, but if library staff doesn't stay on top of these things, the public will have to come to a dirty building, which is never a good thing.

SMOKERS: THE ORIGINAL POLLUTERS

If we see you smoking, we will assume you are on fire and take appropriate action.

—Douglas Adams

For several very good reasons and one very bad one, the number of people who use tobacco products is declining. Many states and cities now have laws and ordinances to regulate tobacco use in public places. It's likely that some form of tobacco-use legislation already protects your library; but it's a good idea to reinforce it with a policy of your own to define the restrictions in your own facility.

Your tobacco-use policy can be more restrictive than the prevailing no-smoking laws, but never more lenient. It should clearly define where smoking is permitted on or near the premises, and where it's prohibited. The consequences should be listed including revocation of library use privileges for willful repeat offenders. Remember, you're not restricting someone's personal choice to use tobacco; you're only restricting where it's used, or not used, in and around the library. Tailor your policy to the specific needs of your library, but let the existing laws do the heavy lifting.

The old adage, "where there's smoke, there's fire," certainly applies here. Be alert to that distinctive whiff of smoke, any smoke really, and investigate immediately. It's important to locate the source of the smoke as quickly as possible, because not only is the smoke a concern, any hastily hidden evidence can result in fire. Smokers attempting to sneak quick cigarettes often seek quiet, secluded corners near vents or windows, or light up in places like restrooms or offices. Stairwells and service corridors are also popular, out-of-the-way places for Smokers to pause.

Instruct your staff on effective ways to discourage smoking inside the library and in public areas outside the facility. They should also be prepared to respond appropriately when confronted with anger or belligerence. Rehearse a variety of scenarios of people ignoring the no-smoking policy and discuss the likely outcomes.

Be aware of people smoking too near the entryways to the library. Smoke concentrated in these often-sheltered areas creates an unpleasant, pungent atmosphere for customers arriving and leaving through the entrances. Placing "No Smoking" signs at strategic locations makes customers aware that smoking tobacco is something actively and expressly prohibited in the facility.

Learn your state and local smoking restrictions. What is the minimum distance smoking is permitted outside public buildings? Some places ban smoking entirely in all public areas, even outside. Depending on your laws, consider placing receptacles for the proper disposal of smoking materials at the legal distance outside the library entrance. This will allow responsible Smokers to dispose of their materials as they approach the building, and will help minimize litter in the entryway.

Sometimes you may discover that the clandestine Smokers in your library are minor children experimenting with tobacco. In most states, it's illegal for children under the age of 18 to purchase tobacco products, but the possession of tobacco isn't regulated as closely, if at all. Know your community and your customers. Many parents of these children aren't aware their child is experimenting with tobacco. The overindulgent parents may actually tolerate smoking as their child's form of self-expression like a Mohawk haircut, only unhealthy.

Choose the best course of action to protect your library and your customers. Dispense discipline carefully because these are someone else's children. If you're able to confiscate the smoking materials, offer to return them to the parents during their next library visit. Be especially concerned about the matches and lighters, because children who experiment with smoking may also experiment with fire.

Your "No Smoking" policy applies to the library's staff, too, particularly where smoking is also regulated by law. Turning a blind eye to employees smoking on the premises only undermines the credibility of your no-smoking policy and sets an unfair double standard. If you think no one notices the smell, you're kidding yourself. Of course, the tobacco police aren't going to show up in riot gear to enforce the smoking ban, but your customers will not tolerate the indifference for long. They expect and deserve a safe, clean, smoke-free environment. Don't give them a reason to stay away, or worse, take their patronage elsewhere.

In Summary

For this problem customer, your greatest advantages are your state and local smoking laws and ordinances. Rely on those to give your nonsmoking rules authority. Investigate any smell of smoke immediately and take appropriate action. This goes for your staff, too. Be particularly alert for minors experimenting with smoking materials, as this may also pose a fire hazard and more may be going on than simple curiosity. This is discussed in greater detail in Part VII "Arsonists and Other Pyromaniacs: For the Love of Fire."

SQUEAKY WHEELS AND OTHER NITPICKERS: YOUR RUNNING COMMENTATORS

> Man invented language in order to satisfy his deep need to complain.
>
> —Lily Tomlin

You know the Squeaky Wheel. You've seen her in grocery stores, department stores, and even doctors' offices. Unfortunately, she also has a card to your library, and she uses it with regularity. This person has an axe to grind, and she wants the world to know what it is. She complains to people who have the misfortune to stand by her in line while she vents. She sometime gets so loud that her complaints soar past the reference or circulation desk.

Many Squeaky Wheels have a propensity for hyperbole. The Squeaky Wheel didn't deserve that overdue notice; she turned in that DVD days before it was due. She's been waiting too long, months, for a reserve book (even though it was published only two weeks ago). Your staff is so slow she's been standing in line most of the afternoon, and now her feet are so swollen she'll need new shoes. Most of all, she doesn't like the way that rude circulation person looked at her.

Sometimes the most annoying Squeaky Wheel is the Whiner, who is also apparently a customer who cannot be satisfied. No matter what you do or how hard you work, nothing is good enough. At one library a Whiner came in five minutes before closing and returned over $600 in "presumed-lost" materials. Then she started whining about having to pay the overdue fine. The circulation clerk said she wasn't authorized to waive any fines, so the woman insisted on speaking to someone in authority who would "do the right thing." By then, it was closing time, and everyone she could appeal to had left for the day. The Whiner was still insistent, even though the staff member kept telling her, truthfully, that she didn't have the authority to waive the fines. The Whiner was the last patron to leave the building, but she came back as soon as the library opened the next day with the same demand. The director backed the staff member, and the woman reluctantly paid her fines.

Unfortunately, people have learned that the Squeaky Wheel or Whiner often gets the best service. Their bad behavior gets them fast service; it's just human nature to want them, and their problem, to go away.

As hard as it is, when you deal with a Squeaky Wheel, be calm. Be professional, and listen to their complaints patiently, because, after all, they are still your customers. If you can't satisfy their demands, offer them a suggestion form and tell them honestly that their concerns will be looked into. On some occasions, their complaints are valid, and those should be dealt with immediately. Be sure to communicate to the Squeaky Wheel or Whiner that the problem has been rectified. However, don't let them go to the front of the line or have special privileges just to get them to stop squeaking.

In Summary

Squeaky Wheels have learned that the louder they complain, the faster they will be dealt with. Although it is tempting, very tempting, to ignore everyone else and deal with the Squeaky Wheel just to get them to go away, you must not do it. After they've waited their turn, listen patiently to their complaint, and let them know that you'll look into it. They might want to put it in writing, too. The Squeaky Wheels and Whiners, as annoying as they are, are still your customers, and they should be dealt with as professionally as all others.

TEXTERS: THE MEDIUM IS THE MESSAGE

People have entire relationships via text message now, but I am not partial to texting. I need context, nuance and the warmth and tone that can only come from a human voice.

—Danielle Steel

The Texter is a new breed of rude customers. Usually teens or young adults, these people stop texting just long enough to ask their questions, and then quickly ignore you, turning once again to their texting. You can basically forget about any sort of reference interview.

What you feel like doing is grabbing the cell phone and putting it in your desk drawer or, let's be honest, throwing it across the room until the reference transaction is complete.

Several ways are available to deal with the Texter:

- You can let the person text in peace and hope you've gotten the request right.
- You can ignore the behavior and interrupt his texting to ask any questions you might need to clarify his request.
- You can wait to access the database, open a book, or do anything to answer the question until the texting stops. Eventually, the Texter will realize you're not doing anything about his request. If this epiphany is taking too long, you might cheerfully announce, "Just let me know when you're ready."

However, be prepared for eye-rolling and heavy sighing. We have to admit. The last solution on the list is our favorite. As we've said before, librarians aren't saints!

In Summary

Texters are the new face of rudeness. They want your help, and then act as if you aren't even there while they text their BFF about their latest OMG moment. You can leave them alone and hope you're looking for what they actually want. You can interrupt them for clarification. Or you can wait until they've finished texting before you begin work on their question.

TIME-CHALLENGED PATRONS: "I STILL HAVE A MINUTE BEFORE YOU CLOSE"

> You may delay, but time will not.
>
> —Benjamin Franklin

You start the warnings early. At 8:45 P.M., your recorded message "The library will be closing in fifteen minutes" plays over the speakers. At 8:50 P.M., your message goes on again: "The library will be closing in ten minutes. It you are working on a computer, please begin to save your work." At 8:55, your message announces, "The library will close in five minutes. Please be sure to take all of your things with you when you leave." You might even flick the lights off and on a couple of times. Then at 9:00 P.M., the message you've waited all day for: "The library is now closing. Thank you for coming." The last customer hurries to save his document, and you escort him to the door.

Just as you begin to lock up, a man pushes past you into the library. You tell him the library is closed. He insists that your clocks are wrong, that it is 8:59, and he still has the right to come in.

You tell him that it is closing time, and the computers have been shut down for the night. You invite him to return in the morning. You give him a bookmark with library hours on it and tell him that the online resources are available round the clock.

He says that he just has to check out one book and it will only take a minute. He says you can write down the information and input it in the morning, when the computers are back up.

You've never seen this man before. Your staff is gathered at the circulation desk, waiting for him to leave so they can go home perhaps because your library is in a high-crime neighborhood, and the rule is that everyone leaves together. This is only one example among other problems. If the staff stays after closing, you need to pay the hourly employees overtime which you don't have in your budget. Also, there's an automatic alarm that will arm itself in 13 minutes.

You can handle this in one of several ways:

- You can run and get the book if he remembers where it is, and if it isn't checked out. However, this sets a bad precedent, and if you do it for one person, you have to be fair and give your other customers the same consideration.
- You can firmly remind him the library has closed and staff is on their way out.
- If he still refuses to go, you can ask him calmly, "Are you ready to leave now or shall I call the police to escort you out?"

However, do not offer to stay behind by yourself, especially since you have no idea who this man is; and, if you break the "everyone leaves at one time" rule, some staff will see it as an opportunity to leave by themselves when they want to. The risk and liability are just too great.

One case in which you *do* need to stay with your library customers is when children are left after hours. You can't leave a child alone outside an empty building. For that matter, you can't leave them inside an empty building. Parents might be delayed in picking up their child because they're caught in traffic, or they're confused about library hours. When staff determines that a child is alone, every effort should be made to try to locate the child's parent. Staff should call any available contact numbers to reach the parent or other family member who can come to the library and get the child. If this fails, or the child is too young to give you parental information, you need to contact the police department as soon as possible. <u>Never leave a child alone in the building or alone outside after the library closes, and always have two staff members stay with him or her</u>. The bottom line is that when dealing with closing the library, policies and procedures need to be in place and followed.

In Summary

No matter how many "The Library Is Closing" warnings you give, there are always those Last-Minute and Last-Second Patrons who refuse to leave. They can be extremely tenacious, and sometimes, security needs to be brought in. Policies and procedures should address library closing rules, including whether staff leaves alone or as a group. Children left after hours are a special circumstance. If you're unable to locate the parents or guardians, contact the police department. Two staff members should stay with the child until someone arrives for them, and never leave them alone, inside or out.

PART III

It's All about Me

ARGUERS AND BULLIES: THE AGGRESSIVE CUSTOMERS

If you are neutral in situations of injustice, you have chosen the side of the oppressor.

—Desmond Tutu

When you think about it, anyone can become a Bully. It's easy. All you have to do is the following: (1) allow your ego to bloat beyond rock star proportions, (2) sell your puny soul to the devil, (3) inflict your clever superiority on others, and then (4) revel in the *schadenfreude*. No guilt. No remorse. No responsibility for the consequences.

Bullying has become a serious problem in recent years. Because bullying is such irresponsible behavior, it's mostly attributed to children and teens who lack the maturity to realize how inappropriate it is. However, there are adults who engage in this behavior too. Bullies of all ages derive power, satisfaction, and even cruel entertainment in the intimidation and humiliation of others.

Bullies gain even more advantage in the normally quiet, peaceful confines of the library where their hostility gains even greater traction. No one likes to create a scene, except, of course, Bullies. To them, creating a scene is the whole point because they know their victims aren't likely to offer any resistance just to avoid the foofaraw. They enjoy their victim's discomfort and the more humiliating the encounter, the better. What's worse, after Bullies get their way, the precedent is set for more confrontations in the future.

Teens bullying in groups tend to be particularly bold. At our library, a group of teens once gathered outside the library entrance to chant taunts at customers as they passed. "You're ugly! You're ugly! You're ugly!" "You're old! You're old! You're old!" It didn't matter who their victims were, they found something to embarrass everyone, and then laughed like a pack of hyenas at the reactions. It made their victims and others who witnessed the taunting feel extremely uncomfortable and many complained to staff.

Offensive activity like this requires immediate and decisive action to eliminate the threat to customers and preserve the reputation of the library. (See Appendix D.) Bullies aren't known for their bravery; and in the case of our shouting teens, we asked our community police officers to take a walk over to the library. A well-placed glare, and the Bullies left as quickly as they appeared.

Staff should also be alert for bullying among younger children in the children's department. While it isn't the librarian's place to discipline the Bully, action should be taken to protect the innocent victims. Remain calm and use respectful behavior when confronting Bullies. This is often enough to discourage their hostile behavior and restore order until their parents can be located to retrieve them. If necessary, separate Bullies from the other children to prevent more episodes. Notify other staff to locate the parents and bring the matter to their attention as tactfully as possible. It's likely this wasn't their little Bully's first performance, but letting unruly children get away with abusive behavior only encourages them to try it again.

Adult Bullies in the library use their aggressive behavior to coerce and intimidate staff or other customers into doing things their way. Adult Bullies aren't necessarily entertained by the reactions of their victims like their adolescent counterparts. They're more interested in getting a desired result through manipulating people, like your staff. The gratification of seeing others squirm is secondary.

We've had adult Bullies steamroll their way to the front of a long line of customers at the circulation desk. Usually a calm statement, such as "I'm sorry, but this person was next," will keep the line moving in the right order. Be prepared for the Bully to slam his or her materials on the desk and storm out. If this happens, we've found it best to help the next person and ignore the bad behavior.

It may be tempting for staff to compromise library rules, "just this once," to keep the bullying customer happy; but Bullies, once successful, don't stop with once. The only prudent move is to cite your library's policies that clearly define what is and what is not permitted and stick to them.

We've all seen bullying behavior on the road. "Road Warriors," they call them, even though the fighting is one sided. Unfortunately, some people don't leave this attitude in their cars, and you find yourself dealing with a hostile Bully. Once angry, bullying behavior turns aggressive, it's more difficult to manage. Along with finding a resolution, you must also protect yourself, your staff, and even the other customers. Again, a calm, professional demeanor will help keep the confrontation from becoming physical. Aggressive behavior that seems to be escalating should not be dealt with alone. If it becomes necessary, call the police.

Nothing is gained by attempting to handle an out-of-control-situation alone, risking the safety of others. Any bullying that escalates into dangerous, threatening, and even criminal behavior should be reported to the police immediately. While there are no federal regulations that specifically target bullying, state law is on your side. Just about every state has some form of antibullying legislation in place that prohibits bullying, cyberbullying, or both. In the event a library computer is used for cyberbullying, quarantine the machine immediately.

Forms of cyberbullying include threats of violence, stalking, or hate crimes, child pornography, or photos or video taken of someone in a location where the individual would normally expect privacy. Report this type of activity to both the authorities and to the Internet service provider whose terms of service prohibit these transactions. As with any illegal activity, thorough documentation is essential. Your state and local authorities can advise on their specific reporting requirements.

Since the introduction of social media, it's become easier than ever to bully someone. Your library can help combat this growing threat by offering antibullying education to your customers and staff. Local experts in victim assistance may offer workshops on the subject of bullying. You might also develop a bibliography of books and websites that target this type of behavior or feature items from your collection on the topic of bullying. A variety of brochures and educational resources are available online that may be downloaded free of charge.

Even though most state antibullying laws contain some protection, they probably don't include all types of unwanted behavior. Taunting, disrespect, and name-calling aren't crimes, but they don't belong in the library either. Any behavior that is not socially acceptable to reasonable people should be included in your library's comprehensive behavior policy (Appendix D).

When it comes to bullying, the absolute worst thing you can do is pretend it didn't happen. Anna Julia Cooper, an American teacher and writer, once said: "Bullies are always cowards at heart and may be credited with a pretty safe instinct in scenting their prey" (http://www.brainyquote.com/quotes/authors/a/anna_julia_cooper.html).

Aggressive behaviors, such as bullying, create a hostile environment for all library customers, as well as staff. Whether the activity occurs outside the entrance, or inside the facility, intimidating, disrespectful and offensive behavior or language forms a lasting memory of a bad experience. This type of behavior has the potential to trigger a retaliatory response that can escalate into physical violence. Customers aren't likely to return to a place where they were treated badly or where they feel their safety is at risk.

In Summary

Bullying occurs in all age groups, though most often among children and adolescents. The hostile behavior is even more effective in the library where victims tend to comply in order to avoid a scene. Library management must take immediate action to stop bullying incidents, to protect both the customers and the reputation of the facility. Be sure all incidents that occur among children in the youth department are controlled promptly and then reported to the parents. Document the entire incident, including the names of all those involved. When any bullying, including cyberbullying, escalates into threatening or dangerous territory, contact the authorities for help.

CENSORS: THE LIBRARY'S SELF-APPOINTED WATCHDOGS

> Censorship, like charity, should begin at home; but, unlike charity, it should end there.
>
> —Clare Booth Luce

Carol, a young mother, walked into our library clutching a DVD. It was obvious she was unhappy with it. She told the youth librarian she wanted that particular DVD and all other copies of it we owned taken from the shelves. Fortunately, we had a policy and procedure in place that had been approved by administration, the library board, and the city attorney. The librarian listened quietly as Carol ranted, and then gave her a "Material Challenge Form" (see Appendix G) telling her that her concerns were taken seriously. The librarian told Carol that after she submitted the form, a committee would review the video, Walt Disney's *The Brave Little Toaster*, and decide its fate in the children's collection.

The next day, Carol returned to the library with the completed form in hand. She had written: "It sounded innocent and enjoyable for the whole family, but it tends from the very start to teach violence and total lack of self-control. To children, animated objects represent real life beings like themselves. We, the children and I, were convinced we could no longer watch it after only 10–15 minutes of it. I kept hoping words like 'Jerk, idiot, stupid' and such would end but they kept coming . . ."

Carol wrote that it didn't matter what others thought because "I am to give account, as is everyone, to GOD HIMSELF (her capitalization), for how I raise 'my' children." She answered the last question on the Material Complaint Form, "Do you feel another individual has a right to censor your library Material?": "Is there not a 'standard' of Bible in our country anywhere anymore. God forgives if we repent. 'Rights' come from Christian foundations in America over 200 yrs. ago."

Carol, in all her righteous indignation, believed that she was doing the right thing by getting *The Brave Little Toaster* removed from our library collection. Ironically, from her comments, it was obvious that, although she felt she could make this censorship decision for other parents, she believed they had no right telling her what her children could or couldn't watch. In our experience, most censorship requests are aimed at the children's department, a majority of them based on that person's religious beliefs.

Of course, not all censorship attempts against children's material come from a person's religious or moral values. We had one mother insist we pull the Smurf books because the Smurfs are blue, and children would find that "confusing." The complaint sounded ridiculous, but this woman was serious, and acted as though the books would be extremely harmful to children. Every censorship attempt, no matter how odd it might seem to you, needs to be taken seriously, and your library's policy and procedures need to be followed.

Sometimes, organizations lead censorship attempts. School and public libraries in our area were targets of a right-wing group on a mission to get all Shel Silverstein titles eliminated from library collections. They believed that since Silverstein was gay, children who read his books would follow that lifestyle, too. Members of this group would "testify" at public meetings, displaying the artwork in Silverstein's books, pointing out things that might represent homosexuality. Fortunately, they failed, but countering their efforts was a herculean endeavor.

Liberal groups may also want books removed from the collection. They have targeted such titles as *Little Black Sambo*, *Nappy Hair*, and *Huckleberry Finn*. Everyone has books and movies they don't like. It's just that not everyone tries to influence what other people read or watch.

Some librarians have problems with people objecting to books and DVDs that have sexual content. One of our strongest complaints in this area dealt with one of the older Longarm westerns, *Longarm and the Hangman's Noose*. While there are hundreds of Longarm titles, the person who complained only wanted that one particular book removed.

No matter how professional librarians try to be during censorship efforts, some situations have the potential to become emotional when someone wants a book removed for personal reasons. Our worst experience, hands down, was when a mother brought in a blood-splattered copy of Derek Humphry's

Final Exit: The Practicalities of Self-Deliverance and Assisted Suicide for the Dying that she had found beside her dead son's body. She'd brought a picture of his bloody corpse to show us how dangerous this book was, especially for younger adults; he was in his early twenties. It was such a tragic experience that everyone involved ended up crying. This was not the time or the place for our "Material Complaint Form." This wasn't the time to correct her and say that *Final Exit* advocates against gun-related suicide." In the end, we didn't replace the copy at that particular branch, but there were other copies in the system.

Sometimes, Censors take matters into their own hands. In one library, someone had gone through many of the art books and carefully cut out almost all of the depictions of nudes. However, staff never figured out whether it was a Censor or a thrill-seeker.

Censors might check out and keep materials they feel are unfit for a public library and pay the "lost" fines and replacement fees. In cases of a group of people targeting a specific title this way, the book disappears as soon as the replacement hits the shelves, so it's almost impossible to provide that title for library customers. However, these "watchdogs" probably don't consider themselves censors.

So who are the "typical" Censors? They are female, male, religious, nonreligious, conservative, liberal, old, young; but lest we pat ourselves on the back as the ultimate protectors of the written word, sometimes, we have met the enemy, and in the words of Pogo, "He is us." We use selection and deselection to pick and choose what goes onto our shelves. We choose "literary fiction" over the more popular romance fiction for the good of our customers, of course. The "balanced" collection is one of the great myths of librarianship.

Your staff needs to know that in material challenges, they have the backing of their administration. Ironically, people in a library's chain of command can become Censors. Several years ago, a city official noticed a copy of *Lesbian Nuns* in one library's book sale area. He mentioned to the library director that he wanted it removed immediately. The director knee-jerked and not only threw out the offending tome, but also had staff "evaluate" all books in the library that had to do with gay or lesbian issues. In the real world, politics often trump intellectual freedom.

You have an almost a 100% guarantee that sometime in the life of your library, someone will try to censor something. Because of this, it is vital to be prepared for material challenges:

1. Develop a policy and a procedure to deal with material challenges. A good place to start is the American Library Association's "Intellectual Freedom Toolkits": http://www.ala.org/offices/ oif/iftoolkits/intellectual. Here, you will find just about everything you need, from "Intellectual Freedom and Libraries: an Overview" to "Preparing for and Responding to Challenges." Your procedure should include a "Library Material Complaint" form (Appendix G).
2. Get buy-in at all levels, and make sure all approvals: library management, city or county administration, and legal department, library board, among others, are in place. You also need staff buy-in, because they are the first responders to the complaints. Training is essential, and everyone needs to remember that neutrality is vital.
3. Establish a committee of staff and someone from the public to evaluate materials complaints.
4. Always have a Library Material Complaint or Material Reconsideration form on hand at all public desks. Information should include:

   - Name and contact number of person making the complaint
   - Name of staff person receiving complaint
   - Time and date of complaint
   - Name of material being challenged
   - Reason for challenge
   - Action taken (including committee decision, if necessary)
   - Date and time of patron notification
   - Name of staff who notified patron
   - Additional comments and/or questions
   - Need for additional follow-up

Sometimes, customers are satisfied with just having their opinions about materials heard by staff. Sometimes, they want action. Materials challenges are all a little different, and need to be approached on a case-by-case basis. However, there is always a need to follow procedures, and it is vital to communicate the final decision to the person making the complaint.

President John F. Kennedy once said, "If this nation is to be wise as well as strong, if we are to achieve our destiny, then we need more new ideas for more wise men reading more good books in more public libraries. These libraries should be open to all—except the censor." We wouldn't go so far as to suggest that Censors be banned from libraries, but we do know that if you don't have a defense in place, you are putting your collection at risk.

In Summary

Anyone, liberal or conservative, can be a Censor. Many are parents protecting their children and other children from materials they deem offensive. Some want materials removed based on their own religious beliefs. Others object to having parts of their organization's or religion's beliefs shared with the general public. Sometimes, people object to the lifestyle, political views, religious beliefs, and other aspects of the author, and don't think his or her works should be included in library collections. Libraries should have a strong challenged materials policy that has been approved by their management, board, and legal department to fend off censorship attempts.

"I-KNOW-SOMEONE-IMPORTANT" CUSTOMERS: THE NAME-DROPPERS

> Pussycat, pussycat, where have you been?
> I've been up to London to visit the Queen.
>
> —Songs for the nursery, 1805

> "I know the mayor. Personally."
> "I'll just talk to my councilperson about that."
> "The library director is a friend of mine. A *good* friend."

Oh, those Name-Droppers, the people who wield their influential acquaintances like weapons. Lacking real power of their own, they threaten you with someone else's in order to get you to do things their way. Name-dropping is a bullying tactic intended to intimidate you. Don't fall for it. In our experience, pompous name-dropping is a bluff, tantamount to the triple dog dare. Unless you've done something willful and egregious to the Name-Dropper, the mayor isn't going to call and the library director won't demand your resignation. In fact, they may not even know this customer.

You really have no way to prepare for Name-Droppers. You never know when one will show up and drop a name on you for some perceived violation of their ultimate library experience. Ordinarily, the staff makes every effort to please customers and treat them with respect, but sometimes disagreements are unavoidable no matter how hard they try.

Wouldn't it be wonderful to answer every request with a "yes?"

Unfortunately, library policies sometimes require answers to be "no": not this time, not in here, not until you pay your past due fees. Most customers simply accept these terms and go about their business unperturbed. Name-Droppers see "no" as a challenge, a way to test your resolve, to see if you can be influenced or intimidated into breaking policy, or creating a special policy just for them. They may attempt to negotiate a bit at first, hoping you'll do things their way, but when that fails, they become frustrated. Unable to manipulate you on their own, they drop names of people with power, people they hope you fear.

This rude behavior does not change the level of service this customer is entitled to receive. When you reach an impasse with a Name-Dropper, even if you're unable to satisfy their demands completely, look for an opportunity to compromise. Whenever possible, determine an amicable solution that will allow both the customer and the staff to part as friends. Understandably, this isn't always possible. The solution chosen should be something that could also be offered to any other customer. Making an exception for this customer creates a dangerous precedent you'll have to live with for years to come. Be careful not to create a bigger problem while trying to solve this one.

It's imperative you maintain your composure with irritated Name-Droppers. It may be tempting to trump their VIP list with your own, more important names, or comment that you know the same dignitaries they do. While this sounds like great fun, it is counterproductive and unprofessional to provoke any customer. Your focus is resolving this library transaction in a manner consistent with library policies. Inciting them in any way only compels them to tell their prestigious friends all about your rude behavior and bad customer service, and you *will* hear about that. Remain professional.

Unlike their angry counterparts, peaceful Name-Droppers use their powers for good. These are actually some nice folks to know. They too have prestigious friends. They want you to know that, and possibly offer you some enlightenment or assistance. They want to help.

Their high-powered connections tend to bolster their confidence to dispense advice, inspiring them to tell you better ways to manage your library or arrange your collection. Their suggestions are meant to be helpful, even though they may contradict everything you know as a college-educated librarian. Some of their suggestions may actually have merit. Your Name-Dropper will appreciate knowing if you intend to look into any of their ideas, but don't make promises. Even if you never do a thing with their advice, they will derive a sense of civic accomplishment from having passed along their wisdom to you. Unlike the angry type of Name-Dropper, it isn't all about them.

If their high-level associations are genuine, these well-connected individuals are powerful allies. They tend to be very civic minded and active in the community, which is how they came to know a lot of local officials in the first place. Building positive relationships with these customers provides a conduit to their friends, the elected officials who make your funding decisions. Having your library's needs confirmed and validated to them by these customers can be very advantageous at budget time.

In Summary

For the Name-Dropper, the word "no" can be a challenge and an invitation to test your resolve and composure. It's a bullying tactic to intimidate you into letting them have their way. Let your policies be your guide and don't be coerced into breaking them. Compromise whenever possible, but remember that any courtesy you offer one customer, you must also offer to others. Peaceful Name-Droppers, on the other hand, can be your library's greatest allies. Their influential connections may prove valuable at budget time.

VIPS: FLAUNTING THEIR SELF-IMPORTANCE

A great man is always willing to be little.

—Ralph Waldo Emerson

A local dignitary, who is a major funding proponent of your library, approaches the reference desk. He extends his hand and greets the librarian, making certain she understands this is no ordinary customer. He asks her if the library has a particular reference item, which it does. The librarian locates the item for him and as he flips through the pages, he says this is exactly what he needs. However, being a very busy man, he explains he doesn't have time to stay and do his research in the library. He asks if he could check it out and take it with him to his office. The librarian knows this VIP, and as much as she would like to oblige him, she knows this is a heavily used text, and library policy clearly states that reference items are not to be circulated. It even says this, right on the book's label. So here's the question: What's the best way to handle special VIP requests?

Political savvy is an important skill for library staff that work with public officials. Cultivating a positive working relationship with your VIPs makes your library an important resource, one they can count on, with a staff they might regard as friends. This can pay dividends at budget time; but before you begin making exceptions for your VIPs, be aware that doing so can have unintended consequences.

In an ideal world, there is no hierarchy among library customers; each customer is a VIP. Everyone shares the library's bounty in relative peace and harmony, according to clearly defined and equally applied library policies. It doesn't take long to disrupt this harmony once the word gets out you're playing favorites with certain customers, more "important" customers.

When you start making exceptions, things can get out of hand. Where do you draw the line? If you bend the circulation policies for the mayor, does that same courtesy apply to his family members? What happens when his daughter comes in with a last-minute school project? Next come the city manager and council members. If the mayor gets special favors, surely they should get them, too. You certainly don't want to slight anyone in this important governing group. Before long, the dignitaries' friends will be playing their VIP cards, because they were told you might excuse a fine, or extend a rental. If one or two rules can be bent for so many, surely there's wiggle room in the others too. Pretty soon your entire policy manual is nothing more than a three-ring doorstop.

A library manager who decides to entertain a VIP list places the staff in an awkward position, especially if staff is not authorized to break policies. When a dignitary arrives expecting preferential treatment because the manager had made an exception in the past, the staff may not be as willing to oblige them today. It undermines staff's faith in policies that aren't applied equally, and it's very uncomfortable when challenged by other customers. The manager must be prepared to deal with the potential fallout of favoring dignitaries.

Some VIPs can be very persuasive. Their reasons for bending the rules may be perfectly legitimate and their expectation of having their request fulfilled can be quite intimidating to staff. We've found it very effective for the library manager to handle dignitary requests personally, or assign a specific, politically savvy staff member to assist them. Referring these requests to a VIP liaison, and in many cases, that's someone from library administration, ensures that each dignitary receives consistent service.

In answer to our opening question, the manager or VIP liaison should have the authority to say "no" to checking out any reference items. Instead, if staffing permits it, consider allowing the liaison to perform the VIP's research for him, if that's acceptable to him. Ultimately, the manager has the final word on how business is conducted in the facility.

Some VIPs may shamelessly use their status or title to gain preferential treatment. They expect more comprehensive service than they perceive other customers receive. Of course, every customer already gets superb customer service, no matter what their social status. The privileged VIPs have to wait for their turn like everyone else. Those who demand specially expedited service, which is an unfortunate political reality, might gently be reminded that the library is a shared community asset with thousands of taxpayer customers. It simply isn't ethical to neglect these customers and always favor others. Your policies should back this up, provided you enforce them to the letter.

Despite all of this talk of consistency and fair treatment for all, experienced librarians know high priority, rush projects for VIPs are inevitable. Most VIPs are reasonable people who remember that the folks around them are voters. It's political suicide to demand special treatment over their constituents, who may carry a grudge all the way to the next election.

Other times the VIP's request for vital information truly cannot wait. Handle these projects on a case-by-case basis, assigning staff and resources as appropriate to expedite the request. By coming through in a clutch, your library and staff will leave a very positive impression, even though your only reward may be another rush project. If you aren't able to accommodate their request, explain this and suggest other sources they may consult for the information. If you can't fix their problem, at least help them find someone else who can. One good thing, today's electronic resources have alleviated some of these access problems.

Perhaps the most challenging dignitary is the VIP Wannabe (VIPW). VIPWs are individuals with a little fame and a lot of ego, whose most distinguishing characteristic is asking, "Don't you know who *I* am?!" Unfortunately, the answer is usually "no."

Unlike high-profile VIPs and elected officials, the VIPWs have the advantage of being able to offend people with abandon. They expect their limited celebrity to gain privileges not afforded to others, and they aren't afraid to demand it; but that performance doesn't play at the library. It can be challenging to satisfy VIPWs and maintain your professionalism. Rude, obnoxious behavior should not be tolerated, and asking them to leave is an option. Corrective actions for bad customer behavior should be defined in your policies what you deem appropriate for your library with approval from your legal department. Be firm, be straightforward, be patient.

No amount of celebrity, real or perceived, deserves preferential treatment. We'd like to believe that every member of the Rock and Roll Hall of Fame could parade into our library right now and the service they'd receive would be no different than the next regular customer in line. The library is for all the people, equally, all the time, and it needs to stay that way.

In Summary

Occasionally, when VIPs visit the library, some may ask or even expect you to make exceptions to library policies to accommodate their busy schedules. Remember, there can be no hierarchy among customers, even the ones who probably control your purse strings. When you make exceptions for certain customers you invite problems and undermine your policies. After you bend the rules for one VIP, it may be difficult to stop the unintended chain reaction of favors for others. With a little political savvy you can create win-win outcomes for your VIPs by suggesting compromises that will deliver the results they need without compromising your policies.

"I-PAY-YOUR-SALARY" CUSTOMERS: THE LESS THAN BENEVOLENT BENEFACTORS

> Max Troy: Now, listen to me, Cop. I pay your salary.
> Sgt. Joe Friday: All right, sit down. I'm gonna earn it.
>
> —*Dragnet*, 1954 television show

It's a strange dichotomy. Communities love their libraries. Libraries are points of pride, proof of their community's success and elevated quality of life. Citizens will go to battle to protect their libraries, voicing their unwavering support. Yet sometimes, these same crusaders, when irritated, will treat the library staff with complete contempt. They insult the employees and demean their service with pompous comments like "I pay your salary." People, where's the love?

Smug attitude aside, these customers make a good point. Taxpayers *do* pay staff salaries. This is why quality customer service is so important. The efforts of the hard-working library staff are what make the library a seamless, pleasant experience for customers. The place can't operate without them. The collection is orderly and well maintained, the facility is comfortable and safe, and programs are expertly prepared. It takes a lot of work to maintain consistently satisfied customers, considering the variety of problem patrons you have to contend with each day.

When a customer reminds you, "I pay your salary," you might just be dying to reply, "Then I'd like to ask you for a raise." We know one librarian who figured how many people lived in the library service area, and then divided her salary by that population. It turned out to be a bargain at 33 cents a year per capita.

Customers who lecture and spout sanctimonious clichés have a lot in common with angry name-droppers. They're frustrated and resort to scare tactics to manipulate and control. These customers can do little more than taunt, and they realize this. As a fellow taxpayer, it may be tempting to reply, "What a coincidence. I'm a taxpayer. I guess I pay my salary too!" Unfortunately, any defensive reply will only escalate an already-tense situation. It may be difficult not to react, but to quote the supercomputer, Joshua, from the movie, *War Games*, "The only winning move is not to play."

To prepare staff for this or any type of difficult customer, consider role-playing scenarios. It's an educational and fun way to prepare them for the eventuality they become targets of these difficult patrons. It's very likely they will at some time in their careers. Knowing your staff is prepared and coached on how to react appropriately can avoid bigger problems in the future.

Many times a customer is truly provoked into making the "salary" comment. It should never be dismissed, or even taken lightly. You may have a customer service issue that needs to be addressed. Try to get to the heart of the complaint and take an appropriate course of action. Showing immediate interest in the confrontation demonstrates your concern to both the customer and your employee.

If the complaint truly stems from an employee's poor service or inappropriate behavior, intervene to resolve the customer's complaint. Assist them with their library transaction, completing it to their satisfaction. Be sure the customer understands, this is not the type of service you condone and they can expect to receive far better service in the future.

Once the customer is taken care of, it's time to resolve the issue with the employee. As always, do this away from the public area. Never discipline an employee in front of customers or other staff. After the discussion, be sure to take a few minutes to document it. You may need to refer to this incident in the future if the unprofessional behavior keeps occurring. At some point, if disciplinary action becomes warranted, you will be able to justify your decision with this written account of the employee's actions.

Now more than ever, taxpayers and the always-watching media are scrutinizing the service and behavior of public employees. We're often portrayed in the headlines as overpaid, lazy, greedy, and selfish people who don't deserve their pensions. With this jaundiced point of view, is it any wonder the community questions our worth? No one but the employees can change this perception, and they can do so with consistently excellent, caring, customer service, **every time**.

Each member of our city's workforce is trained from the beginning that every taxpayer in the community is his or her boss. It's important to remember this, knowing any unproductive time on the job, or even perceived idle time, however brief, invites scrutiny. Staff should be highly discouraged from using their smartphones and other devices on the public floor. It gives the appearance of goofing-off on the job, even if it was just a quick text to one of the kids.

However, it's unreasonable to expect employees to neglect their families during work hours. Sometimes these communications are truly necessary. Staff should know to step away from the public area to make these contacts. You never know who might be watching.

All customers deserve our very best, professional, and courteous service every time they visit the library. They should be made to feel that it's a pleasure to serve them. They need to think that their experience was enjoyable and their time well spent. The customers who make unreasonable demands or expect special treatment forget that it would be a disservice to the rest of our customers or our administrative customers, our bosses, to play favorites and reward their rude behavior.

Rely on your written policies. They're your best defense against unreasonable customers. These guidelines define how library transactions are to be conducted to maintain consistency and fairness for all users, and there should be no exceptions made because someone dropped a name. Your policies may not stop the "boss" from ranting, but you'll know you're standing on principle, and every other happy customer within earshot will agree with you.

In Summary

Remember and respect that the customers, also known as the taxpayers, do pay our salaries. Don't dismiss the "I pay your salary" comments or underestimate the determination of a frustrated customer. Excellent customer service is the best way to prove that you and your staff are worth every cent. Use role-playing to prepare staff to accept and react appropriately to this criticism. Remind staff to attend to personal business away from public areas. You never know who might be watching.

IMPATIENT, TYPE A PATRONS: THE INSTANT GRATIFICATION/ "I-DON'T-HAVE-TIME-FOR-THIS" CUSTOMERS

He who sows hurry reaps indigestion.

—Robert Louis Stevenson

John is an impatient man. He doesn't like to wait. When John drives, he weaves in and out of traffic, and gets angry when the light turns red before he can go through the intersection. If someone in front of him doesn't make a turn as quickly as he thinks they should, he honks the horn. At the grocery store, he pushes his cart as though he's in an Olympic race, just so he can beat another person to the checkout lane.

John is also one of your library customers. Just because he's in a library doesn't mean that his attitude will change. No matter how hard you're working, he gets impatient with you. Sometimes, he'll actually say, "Would you hurry up?" or "Can't you go any faster?" or "I don't have time for this. I have other things I have to do." Lines send him into a frenzy. You dread telling him there are seven people ahead of him on the reserve list for the newest military thriller.

Impatient Customers don't tolerate anything that slows them down. Delays irritate them. They tend to be difficult to deal with. On the up side, Impatient Customers are some of the easiest for you to read. Even if they don't say anything, Impatient Customers speak volumes through their body language. They might tap their feet, roll their eyes, mutter to themselves, clear their throats, repeatedly look at their watches, or even tap their fingers on your desk.

With their need for instant gratification, these customers are very hard to please. For the Impatient Customer, you can't find what they want fast enough. The lines at the circulation and reference desks are never moving fast enough. Heaven help you if computer response time is slower than they think it should be.

Impatient Customers can have an effect on you and the way you work. Sometimes, you might feel like going slower on purpose, just to annoy them. You are human, too! Many times, however, they make you nervous, and you try to work faster. When you go faster, it's easier to make mistakes, which, in fact, just makes the wait longer.

The best way to deal with an Impatient Customer is to take the high road. Acknowledge that, from their perspective, waiting is a hardship. Try to be sincere about it. Always announce if there's a problem with computer response time, and proactively apologize for the longer wait. Even if this doesn't seem to calm your Impatient Customer, you'll find the other people in line have had computer issues, and tend to be sympathetic about technical difficulties.

Whatever you do, though, don't move the Impatient Customer ahead in line or rush through the requests of your other customers. It just encourages more of the same bad behavior.

In Summary

Impatient Customers are hard to please. Their words and body language might make you so nervous or anxious you feel the urge to rush. Acknowledge that their wait time is a hardship. Apologize for slow computers. However, don't let their impatience and bad attitude affect your service to other customers.

REBELS: PRIDE IN NONCOMPLIANCE

The Earth needs rebels!

—David Icke

The iconic, enigmatic James Dean continues to embody the image of a Rebel. With him, it was an attitude he exuded, punctuated with his unwavering stare. However, Rebels in the library usually have more chutzpah than mystique, and they don't tend to have James Dean's "cool factor."

Rebels feel that rules don't apply to them, so they can't be expected to follow them. They ignore posted behavior policies and other signs that restrict certain behaviors. They often challenge existing rules just because the rules exist. If you have a 10-book limit, they want 12. If you allow half an hour on the computers, they want an hour. To make matters worse, they might be loud in their challenges.

Never assume that the needs of your library or your other customers are obvious to the Rebel. In fact, never assume the Rebel even cares about such things. The Rebel can be a poster child for egocentricity.

When dealing with a Rebel, you need to be a model of good behavior. Even as the Rebel makes demands, try not to be accusatory or confrontational. Be clear and professional about communicating the library's policies and expectations. If you have to, explain the reasons behind the rules, but don't expect the Rebel to pay attention as to why the rules are there. To the Rebel, rules are bad things, meant to be broken.

If you start breaking library rules because a Rebel is acting obnoxiously, and you just want him or her to go away, it's not fair to your other customers. Be even handed when enforcing library rules. Be consistent. Professionalism and patience, maybe all you have left for the day, are the best tools when dealing with a Rebel.

In Summary

Rebels live by their own set of rules. They try to push the boundaries of your library rules, wanting longer checkout periods, more time on the computer, or no limit to the number of items taken home. They can get argumentative, but you need to stay calm and consistent, even when they're "in your face." Don't cave in just to make them go away, but don't be confrontational either. Try to stay calm even if you're on your last nerve.

PART IV

Mommie Dearest and Other Perilous Parents

OBLIVIOUS PARENTS: "WHAT, ME WORRY?"

> . . . the only earthly certainty is oblivion.
>
> —Mark Twain

What is it about libraries that make some parents do things they would never do at home or anywhere else for that matter? Where else would you see a parent balance their baby carrier, baby included, on top of a copy machine? What parent would conceive of turning their infant or toddler loose and unsupervised on the kitchen counter or a restaurant table? And who would even consider allowing little Billy to climb the bookshelves at home? These parents do exist, and all of them are regular customers at our library.

No one wants to see a child hurt, and there is no better protection than the supervision of a vigilant parent. What about those times when parents aren't quite so vigilant? Libraries need to have written policies to define the expectations for parents and staff when it comes to the safety of children in the library.

In a way, we create the problem ourselves. We encourage parents to bring their children to the library. We have entire sections decorated and designated for children. We even offer programs for them and hold summer reading competitions. We love kids, so we need to be prepared.

Parents come to the library for their own entertainment too, and we pride ourselves in making the library experience enjoyable for them. We want them to browse the stacks. We bait them with the latest bestsellers. We encourage them to use our reference services, and at checkout time, we chat with them at the circulation desk. We love parents!

The perfect storm of parental oblivion arises when a vulnerable child and a distracted parent converge.

Mom sets the baby carrier on the coin-op copy machine because she needs to dig through her purse for change. She'd put the carrier on the floor except it's a public place and the floor is probably germy. Plus, she doesn't want anyone tripping over her baby. That makes perfect sense, except it's an invitation to a nasty fall. A busy librarian might not even notice this little drama unfolding; but if it does come to your attention, a few words of caution are in order. In Mom's state of oblivion, she might not have considered the danger.

We actually had a baby fall from the top of our copy machine before we could get to it. The baby wasn't hurt, thank goodness, but the incident was horrifying. We put a big sign on the copier saying, "Do Not Set Babies or Children on the Copy Machine!" and that seemed to work most of the time. If it didn't, staff rushed over to ask the parent to take the baby from the copier, because at that point, we were more aware of the danger.

This is the universal truth about many policies. They are made as a reaction to something that shouldn't have happened but did. Sometimes we think, "Why do we even have to tell someone not to do that? It's just common sense." But we do.

Then there was the Oblivious Father who approached the circulation desk with an armload of books and his toddler in tow. The toddler was overstimulated from a *Dora the Explorer* program he'd just attended. Oblivious Father opted to set the child on the circulation counter so he could keep an eye on his antsy tot. When the matter of overdue fees came up, Dad was instantly distracted. While the circulation assistant tried to explain the fees, Dad was oblivious that the child was teetering on the counter, grabbing for a colorful object just beyond his reach. Fortunately, the staff member grabbed the toddler before he fell. If she hadn't stopped the child's descent into peril, he would have taken a nasty fall, and all before Dad had a chance to react.

This wasn't our first near miss, so with this incident and the one with the baby falling from the copier fresh in mind, we made a "no babies or children on equipment, counters, or other library furniture not designed for seating" policy. We were diligent in its enforcement, although there were indignant parents who complained loudly about it. Their comment being, "I'd never let my kid fall."

The library is furnished and equipped for customers to conduct library business, and most areas are not child-proof, even the children's department. One Oblivious Grandma brought her grandson to the library for a *Time for Tots* program, and afterward, they picked out a few books. As they headed to the circulation desk, Grandma was enticed by the contemporary fiction section, and she veered into the adult stacks for a quick browse. She became so engrossed with our romance collection that she failed to notice her grandson having a little adventure of his own: scaling the stack behind her. After all, most small children love to climb, and what can be more tempting than a ladder of bookshelves? If Grandma hadn't been so oblivious to her grandson's actions, she would have recognized the risk and pulled him off the shelf. Chances are she'd notice eventually when books began hitting the floor, followed by the boy. This didn't happen, thanks to a quick-thinking page shelving nearby. She removed the tot from his perch and gave him to Grandma, who by now was paying attention.

Modern libraries are constructed, arranged, and furnished through layer upon layer of safety regulations; building codes, fire codes, Occupational Safety and Health Administration regulations and Americans with Disabilities Act requirements, and more. The facilities are designed for safety, but your customers are not. It's perfectly human to become distracted, and for this reason, child safety policies are essential to set the ground rules for responsibility.

The quiet, friendly atmosphere of a library creates a sense of comfort and security for customers. It's a sanctuary of learning and entertainment, giving some parents the mistaken impression they can let down their guard. Surely, the caring library staff will protect their child from harm. "It takes a village," right? Unfortunately, the library staff is usually plenty busy, and they can't keep track of every customer all the time.

This is particularly true in the children's section, where there may be dozens of kids of all ages, reading, playing, and practicing their social skills. Often, a well-meaning parent will occupy their child with a puzzle or book, and then make a quick jaunt to the adult stacks without telling the children's librarian. The unsupervised child is left to his or her own devices until Mom or Dad returns, under the assumption that the librarian will assume responsibility in their absence. They are mistaken. The truth is, a lot can happen before they get back.

Every children's librarian knows, during busy library hours, the children's section is like a big box of kittens. It's impossible to keep track of them all or to know whose child is whose. A child could easily wander away in search of Mom or Dad without being missed, even by an older sibling entrusted with his or her care. One unguarded moment is all it takes. What's worse, any adult can stroll in, take a child by the hand and simply walk away without raising suspicion. We wonder if parents would be as trusting with their car keys or credit cards.

Accidents happen. No one escapes childhood without a scratch, but those injuries don't have to happen at the library. Parents assume a certain amount of risk just by bringing their child to a public place. While we can't guarantee their absolute safety, we can minimize the chance of accidental injury.

If you don't already have a child safety policy, check with other libraries to see if you can borrow theirs. With a little tweaking, you can tailor the policy to meet your library's needs. Be sure to communicate this policy to parents so they understand where the boundaries of responsibility lie. By the way, your tone and focus should be about ensuring the safety of the child, not about questioning their parenting skills. To reinforce your no-children-on-the-furniture policy, simple signage will remind parents that the public desks and other fixtures are not build for kids. Discourage parents from leaving children unattended and unsupervised in the youth and children's section. Here again, signage can help make this statement for you.

You might also consider recruiting the help of trusted, reliable volunteers who can wander the stacks and offer assistance, or provide a distraction for children whose parents are engaged in library business. They can also watch that baby while Mom searches for change in her purse.

In Summary

When parents become distracted, they occasionally forget to keep an eye on their children. These parents do careless things they wouldn't normally do, like leaving their children unattended or failing to notice when their curious children do dangerous things. Library staff needs to be vigilant for these times, to keep parents aware when their attention wanders. Discourage parents from leaving young children unattended, even in the children's department. Pages and volunteers working in the stacks may be helpful in spotting wandering children and keeping parents accountable. Child safety policies should be maintained and enforced.

KID DUMPERS: USING THE LIBRARY AS THEIR FREE BABYSITTING SERVICE

All Unattended Children Will Be Given an Espresso and a Free Puppy.
Unattended Children Will Be Sold to the Circus!

—Signs seen in libraries

Libraries that serve large populations of young families are often used by parents as free childcare facilities. With so many fun activities to keep children entertained and with a vigilant librarian nearby, parents feel comfortable leaving their child unattended while they go shopping, run errands, or just enjoy a little "me" time. We encourage parents to bring their children to our many wonderful programs, but we don't want them to leave their offspring, relinquishing all responsibility to us, which usually happens without our knowledge. This is especially true if the child is very young. We've had parents leave kids who were so young they didn't know their own names, let alone their phone number.

It's expected that children at the library will be accompanied by a responsible adult. The trouble with Dumpers is that until it's too late, the library staff has no idea that they've just become responsible for someone's unsupervised child. In fact, it often takes a while to recognize a child who's been dumped. They're too young to have arrived on their own, yet in the whole time the child has been there, no parent has made an appearance. Unfortunately, these children often go unnoticed if they're quiet and well behaved.

When staff determines that a child may have been left unsupervised, every effort should be made to try to locate the child's parent inside the library. If that fails, staff should attempt to call any available contact numbers to reach the parent or other family member who can come to the library and take responsibility for the child. Until they arrive, try to make the child's experience as pleasant as possible. After all, it's not the child's fault for being left behind. If the child is too young to give you parental information, contact the police department as soon as possible.

The abandoned child needs to regard the librarian as a surrogate, a go-to person for anything he or she needs until the prodigal parent returns. Some clever parents actually coach their children on this ahead of time. Make a point of gaining the child's trust while keeping him or her under close supervision. With other patrons seeking assistance, it's impossible to give your undivided attention to the dumped child at all times. Enlist the help of other library staff to monitor the child's activities and whereabouts. In today's litigious world, you should always have at least two staff members assigned to the child to avoid any accusations of inappropriate behavior later.

Any seasoned children's librarian knows how to communicate with children of all ages and keep them occupied. Some children are unable to entertain themselves as long as others, and once they become bored with an activity, it may be difficult to find another to pique their interest. They may also decide they want to go home long before their parent returns. It's important for their time spent at the library to be fun and meaningful. They should look forward to coming back, and not be afraid to cross the threshold.

Including them in a story time program or other scheduled indoor activity with other children will help to pass the time and stave off loneliness and the sense of abandonment. However, be sure the staff members conducting the activity know this child requires their supervision. You can also ask the child to help you pick up library materials in the children's area, or assist you with simple activities at the desk. This will give them a sense of purpose and accomplishment, and keep them busy in your presence.

It can be irritating to be treated as a babysitter. You're already busy, right? Just remember, the child has done nothing wrong. In fact, they're as stuck with you as you are with them! Your issue is with the absentee parent, not the child.

Dumping occurs because parents assume nothing bad will happen at the library. But what if it does? What if the child becomes hurt or sick? Who has the authority to make medical decisions? Does the child have any allergies? We don't know. What if the child wanders from the library?

Child dumping places both the parent and library in a very precarious position. Though most Dumpers don't see the harm in it, leaving a child behind, unattended, in a public place constitutes abandonment. People are angered by parents in the news who leave young children alone at home while they run to the store for a pack of smokes. How is this different?

Be sure the practice of child dumping is addressed in your child safety policy. Clearly define the consequences, including, if necessary, contacting the police. If all efforts to contact the family within a reasonable amount of time fail, or if the parent is somehow delayed past closing time, the only remaining option is contacting the police. We've had cases where even the police couldn't locate the parent.

When the prodigal parent finally returns, take them aside and explain the realities of child dumping. Speak to the parent, preferably apart from the child, so you can be frank about the risks and consequences of dumping. Emphasize that even the most secure library has risks and accidents can happen. Their child needs them to be there. At that time, we give the parent a written copy of our unattended children policy and outline the consequences for future offences.

Tact and professionalism will produce better results than accusations and anger. Document and date all incidents and policy discussions for future reference should you encounter repeat offenders. (See Appendix D.)

We hear you asking, "At what age can children go unattended at the library?" An excellent question! Latchkey kids are a reality of today's economy. Many parents can't afford babysitters.

Some libraries set a minimum age for children allowed to be there without parental supervision. Others employ a policy statement without specifying an age. For example, "if a child appears to be sufficiently capable and mature" is more flexible than a hard number. It assesses the child's ability to function on his own rather than his chronological age. After all, we know nine-year-olds who have more maturity than some adults!

Finally, let the prodigal parent know they are still welcome at the library. Encourage them to return. Except next time, they should stay and enjoy the facility with their child.

In Summary

Some parents and guardians use their local library as a free babysitting service. They drop their children off at the library, leaving them alone to entertain themselves while the parents run errands. At first, library staff may be unaware these children are unattended, but once it's discovered, staff should make every effort to see that these children are safe until their parents or guardians return. The children should remain within sight of the staff and occupied with something to entertain them. They should know they can count on staff for help and protection. If possible, attempt to contact a responsible party or family member to retrieve the child. Never leave these children alone. If library closing time passes before a responsible party returns for the child, notify police, as this child is essentially abandoned. Your safety policy should address Kid Dumpers and define at what age or stage of development children are allowed to be in the library alone.

PERMISSIVE PARENTS: BEGETTING BRATS IS SERIOUS BUSINESS

A child is a curly, dimpled lunatic.

—Ralph Waldo Emerson

Few subjects are as personal and contentious as religion, politics, and parenting. Criticizing any of them is grounds for an argument.

Religion: "Don't tell me what to believe!" We wouldn't dream of it.
Politics: "Don't tell me how to vote!" It's a free country.
Parenting: "Don't tell me how to raise my child!" Okay, but you're clearly not very good at it.

We can overlook some bad behavior. All children have occasional bad days. They're bundles of energy and they get rambunctious. They get cranky and have tempers and get hurt feelings. Don't we all? But their sweet qualities far outweigh their occasional outbursts.

The children whose overindulgent parents don't establish boundaries are the ones that cause us concern. These children are allowed to run free and set their own limitations as if they're mature enough to make those decisions. In their excitable little brains, the absence of "no," means "yes" as they chase and squeal their way through the stacks, disturbing other customers and creating a nuisance. Their unbridled mischief incites other children to join in the fun, creating an even bigger problem. Fortunately, responsible parents respect the library's rules of conduct and restrain their children from running amok.

Permissive Parents are either reluctant to discipline their children, or they don't discipline them on principle, something about not traumatizing fragile psyches or stifling creativity. These parents often attempt to reason with their misbehaving children instead, usually with mixed results.

It's hard to fathom that some excessively Permissive Parents can remain indifferent, no matter how disruptive their children become. Library staff members know reckless children actually present a hazard. We've all seen children racing through the stacks and colliding with other customers, or crouching low playing hide-and-seek, posing a tripping hazard. Turning a blind eye to out-of-control behavior jeopardizes the safe environment of your library. Parents and/or staff must take action to restore order and prevent injury.

The library's rules of conduct or behavior policy (see Appendix D) should include language that addresses the parents' responsibility to control their children's behavior in the library. Expectations should be clearly defined and copies of this policy should be kept in hand for parents who need a refresher. Discipline is the responsibility of the parents. There's only so much that staff can do. The qualifying circumstances should be defined in the behavior policy as well. Holding parents accountable for the behavior of their children is important, but don't overreact to minor outbursts which are easily remedied.

When necessary, staff may interrupt rambunctious children to keep them from hurting themselves or others. The encounter should be nonthreatening but direct, much like a teacher in a classroom.

Encourage the little bundles of energy to settle down and suggest something fun they can do in the children's department instead, like playing a video game or, dare we say it?—reading something. Maintaining a children's department well stocked with a variety of activities for children will entice them inside and keep them there with fun and educational distractions. If children do relocate themselves to the children's department, be sure their parents are aware of it.

Library volunteers who have gone through background checks can be a tremendous help. They can tend to tasks that the librarian may not have time to do: keeping games and puzzles organized, reshelving books, helping to resolve disputes, or finding specific books. They also provide extra sets of eyes to help supervise the young visitors.

A child whose attention is absorbed in a constructive pastime is far less likely to be disruptive. Other customers can now conduct their library business in peace, parents are spared the library policy lecture for their ill-mannered children, and the library staff can focus on more pleasant tasks.

Kids are not known for their tendency to be quiet. However, while chronically disruptive, boisterous, noisy children may not pose a physical threat, they do spoil the library experience for other young customers. Asking parents to intervene in their children's misbehavior should be your first action. Do this as tactfully as possible to avoid giving the impression you're questioning their parenting skills, even though you probably are. Allow them the opportunity to control their children and resolve the situation on their own, with their dignity intact.

You may encounter resistance from parents who are militant about protecting their children's rights. If the parents feel strongly about this and refuse to rein in their children's outbursts, you may need to ask them to leave the library. No one, even a child, has the right to create a public nuisance in the library.

It's never easy to disinvite a customer. Your aim is to restore peace in your library, not create an enemy. If you keep your emotions in check, your customer is likely to respond in the same manner. When you discuss their leaving, try to couch your request as a win-win, giving you and them a chance to make a fresh start. If approached correctly, leaving the library will be their choice. For example:

"You look like you could use a break."

What parent is going to disagree with that? Ease into a casual conversation about their children. Chances are the parents will realize on their own the children's behavior is inappropriate in the library.

They may decide on their own that it's time to leave, which is exactly what you want. If they don't, suggest it in your next helpful comment. "You know, the park outside is a great place for kids to work off extra energy. Do you think they might enjoy that? I'm just afraid they're going to get hurt running through the stacks." You've expressed your concern for their safety and hinted at your desire for the disruptive behavior to stop. Point made.

Depending on the parents' reaction, you can either help expedite their checkout and part as friends, or make your next comment a pointed reference to your behavior policy. Either way, they'll soon be leaving.

Offer to check out their items personally for their convenience (and to hasten their departure). If your library has a supply of bags, place their items in a bag to make them easier to carry. Any small courtesy will soften the blow for people being handed their hat. Do all you can to ensure their trip to the library accomplished what they had intended, and invite them back on a less hectic day.

In Summary

Overindulgent parents who fail to set boundaries create problems for staff and other customers. Don't ignore or tolerate uncorrected rambunctious behavior that poses a hazard to everyone, including the children. Take action to restore order, but remember that discipline is the parents' responsibility. Be tactful but firm, and offer options when possible. Rules of conduct should be clear. Parents who refuse to rein in their children's bad behavior may be asked to leave the library. However, this is not a permanent banishment. Invite them to return at a time when their children aren't as overstimulated.

ABUSIVE PARENTS: PUTTING THEIR CHILDREN IN A WORLD OF HURT

> . . . Stand up with the innocent or go down with the rest.
>
> —Flora Jessop, Church of Lies

The flip side of the Permissive Parent, who lets a child get away with everything, is the abuser, who takes discipline to the extreme. Obviously, because this behavior is illegal in every state, a library policy isn't necessary. Each state regulates how child abuse is reported and handled. In some states, anyone who even suspects child abuse is required to report it to either child protective services or the police. Be proactive in consulting with your local police department for their direction on reporting abusers in your library.

The abuse doesn't have to be physical, and many abusers engage in more than one type. According to Child Maltreatment 2010, a report compiled by the Children's Bureau of the U.S. Department of Health and Human Services, available at Childwelfare.gov, over 17 percent of abused children were physically abused, 9 percent were sexually abused, and 8 percent were psychologically abused. Fifty-seven percent of abused children were seven years old or younger, and there were slightly more girls than boys. The most frequently abused group was infants under one year old. Eighty-one percent of abusers are parents, most often mothers.

Any abusive treatment of a child, such as violent shaking, hitting or kicking, should not be ignored. The sound of shouting in a library is always jarring and attracts attention. When that shouting is directed in anger at a child, or punctuated with profanity or vulgar language, it is abuse. Hurling demeaning, hateful words at a child is as damaging as physical abuse. It should never be tolerated.

Merely asking the shouting parent to quiet down or leave the library is a disservice to the child. It's a sure bet this isn't the first time the child's been abused, and it isn't going to be the last. Be aware that the way the Abusive Parent is confronted could lead to an escalation of their anger, or result in later consequences for the child when there aren't any witnesses. The library incident needs to be resolved, but, in a larger sense, the abuse needs to be stopped. Call for help.

When an incident occurs, depending on the circumstances, it may be necessary to seek both police and paramedic service if the incident involves injury. The dispatcher who takes your call will determine what resources to send based on the details you provide. People who witness abuse, particularly children, are also affected by it. Crisis response services, if available, are invaluable in helping children and other witnesses cope with what they saw.

Library staff must be properly trained and prepared to react when this behavior occurs in the library. Your local police department and Child Protective Services are possible sources for effective training on recognizing child abuse in all its forms, and how to respond to it. All staff and volunteers should receive the training. Dealing with abusers is serious business and is best done with direction from law enforcement or victim assistance professionals. Confronting a furious customer isn't the same as confronting an abuser, who has already demonstrated the potential for anger and violent behavior.

Your primary concern is the safety of your staff and customers, especially the child being abused. Act decisively. Do not hesitate to call 911 and report the abuse, just like you would any other emergency. The dispatcher may coach you on what to do until the police arrive, but having a staff already trained and prepared will ensure everyone responds correctly.

Library staff is also vulnerable to the actions of agitated, Abusive Parents. Any time anger is involved, there is potential for violence. When it becomes necessary to contact the police, you're going to become the "bad guy" for having involved the authorities, although chances are their paths have crossed before. Thorough documentation is essential because the actions of a child abuser are illegal. The police will want to know the details for their report. Staff and customers who witnessed the incident should contribute their observations as well.

While there is no way to prepare for the unpredictable actions of some people, there are child safety measures you can take to help prevent certain types of abuse from happening. For instance, if the library has a restroom in the children's department, restrict its use to children only unless the child is a baby or toddler and the changing station is in there. The only adults who should be allowed to remain in the children's department are the parents. Approach all other adults who linger but don't appear to have business in the children's department and offer assistance and/or point them in the direction of the adult section. Some adults legitimately come to the children's department without children in tow. Some are new readers. Some are finding books for a child. Unfortunately, there are also predators who haunt children's departments, and those are the ones you need to watch for.

Modifications to the physical environment make your library safer for children. Position bookshelves so they provide a clear line of sight to the librarian's desk in the children's room. Shelve items for very young children well inside the department within easy view of the librarian.

Parents of very young children should be required to stay with their children inside the children's area. When they leave, the child should leave with them. Your child safety policy should contain language defining when a child is considered to be old enough, or independent enough, to remain alone in the department. However, under no circumstances should a child younger than your guidelines specify be left alone at the library. Parents must remain on the premises.

According to childwelfare.gov, the federal definition of child abuse is "any recent act or failure to act on the part of a parent or caretaker which results in death, serious physical or emotional harm, sexual abuse or exploitation" or "an act or failure to act which presents an imminent risk of serious harm." A "child" is "a person younger than age eighteen, who is not an emancipated minor," so teens are protected by law, too. Your state statutes may contain additional information on this.

The federal government does not provide definitions for specific types of abuse, such as neglect, and physical, sexual and emotional abuse. These are up to the states to define and enforce. You may consult your state statues or check childwelfare.gov for links to relevant information for your state. In any case, you need to have a zero tolerance policy where child abuse is concerned. A library isn't a perfect place, but it might very well be the only safe haven a child has.

In Summary

We've all seen parents who resort to physical or emotional abuse when disciplining their children. The rough handling, harsh words, and even profanity are troubling to hear and difficult to watch, and should not be tolerated in the library. When parents become abusive to their children in the library, rely on your State child protection laws to govern this crime. Never ignore or tolerate abusive behavior. Report it. Use caution when approaching angry parents. Empathize and remain calm you don't want to make matters worse with sharp tones and accusations. For the sake of the child and your other customers, defuse the situation as peacefully as possible. Call for assistance as the situation warrants, including contacting police or paramedics if necessary. Educate yourself and staff to recognize the various forms of child abuse and the best way to confront abusers until the authorities arrive. Document any instances of abuse. Children are also at risk from other adults. Adopt a policy to restrict visitors to the youth department to only children and their parents. Other adults have no reason to simply hang out in the youth department. Approach them, assist them as needed, and then ask them to return to the adult section.

PART V

Patrons Who Need Social Services

UNEMPLOYED CUSTOMERS: YOUR JOB CAN HELP THEM GET THEIRS

> It's cool to go places where working people are happy.
>
> —Neil Young

Not everyone visits the library for pleasure. Customers looking for work have serious business to conduct. Even people who have never been out of work can appreciate how frustrating the search must be and pray it never happens to them. But for those in this difficult situation, the library is a refuge, a source of hope, and a place they can make real progress in their job hunt.

This is particularly important in tough economic times when jobs are scarce and applicants abound. The networkers have their own connections, and their job hunt is relatively short. For others, the search can take much longer. Their library becomes not only a job-hunting resource, but also a social place to visit during the day to fill the void left by unemployment. Sitting at home, waiting and praying for the phone to ring, gets old.

Many libraries ramp up their job-seeker resources during sluggish economies. This attracts more unemployed people to the facility, customers and noncustomers, and library resources can become quickly monopolized. While it's certainly important to accommodate the important needs of the job seekers, there are other customers to consider. Ensuring ample computer access and table space for everyone can be challenging.

To avoid congestion, consider designating an area specifically for job hunters if space allows. Depending on the demand, relocate a couple of computers with Internet access, word processing, and print capability in this area, and don't forget a supply of low-tech golf pencils and notepaper. Computer usage should be limited so as many customers as possible get the opportunity to browse or word process. Include plenty of seating with job-search references within easy reach. A collection of resume-writing and motivational books may also be helpful. Other items useful to job hunters include metropolitan bus schedules, a bibliography of employment websites, and even the locations of nearby food banks. If the budget allows, replace the bibliography with a simple message board listing the telephone numbers or websites of employment agencies or social service organizations who assist out-of-work clients.

Of course, nothing is stopping job seekers from using any computer in the house, which, as library customers, they are perfectly welcome to do. Having a designated area specially equipped with all of the things they're likely to need, will at least help to ease the congestion in other public areas.

Long-term unemployment can take a toll on a person's emotional well-being. Anger born of frustration may flair unexpectedly and quickly escalate from a shouting match to a physical confrontation. Library staff should be prepared to act and trained to summon security immediately. This may be the last thing the Unemployed Perpetrator needs, but dangerous behavior for any reason should never be tolerated. Your responsibility is to ensure the safety of all your customers. With any luck the altercation will be settled peacefully before security arrives. If not, the authorities will resolve it for them.

The local police department can provide expert information on how to control volatile situations to protect staff and other customers. Documenting threatening behavior is essential (Appendix G). The report should include the name the offender, a description of what happened, and what the staff did about it. If the outburst became dangerous or physical, you'll need statements from others involved for the full report. You'll want to be able to recall the event correctly, and in detail if needed later.

Unemployment can be very isolating, which fuels anger and frustration. Consider creating a support network for Unemployed Customers to provide encouragement and maintain morale. Invite employment agency representatives, social agency counselors, and others to speak at regularly scheduled meetings to provide advice and offer hope. Be sure to include a resume-writing and job-coaching session. If the library lacks the space for this, explore the options for other available, and free, meeting facilities in your community. Centrally located churches, city hall public meeting rooms, and classrooms at city recreation facilities are excellent prospects. Here is where your helpful, well-connected VIPs can be a tremendous asset. With the right motivation, librarians for some facilities may agree to waive their customary room-usage fees for gatherings of this type.

Many unemployed people are accustomed to being busy and productive. Your Unemployed Regulars may even offer to help around the library, looking for something constructive to do. Everyone needs to feel useful. They may see it as a way to show appreciation for the help they've received in their job search. If the library has a policy to register volunteers, invite them to sign up and help them through the process.

Even if they just want to hang out at the library, there's no time limit on how long customers can stay. As long as they're not disrupting staff or other customers, they're perfectly welcome to remain at the library. However, there are limitations to where they can go. The youth department is one of these places.

Library policy should clearly state that parents or their designated representatives are the only adults allowed in the children's section. All staff must enforce this as tactfully as possible. After all, not everyone who wanders into the youth department is a child molester. Unexpected visitors are inevitable in such an inviting wonderland. There are magical things in there, like fanciful artwork and stained glass, rabbits and hamsters, puppets, and sunshine. Who wouldn't like a glimpse of that? To someone who is experiencing the discouragement of unemployment, a nostalgic reminder of a happier time seems irresistible. If you're not busy, there's no harm in giving the ten-cent tour, ending at the youth department exit, of course. This unspoken invitation to leave allows everyone to save face. However, if staffing doesn't permit you this time away from the desk, it may be necessary to approach the visitor and explain the children's area restrictions. Remember, this is not an accusation but a statement of the child safety rules to someone who didn't know.

The loss of one's livelihood is tragic and always difficult. The library may not be able to fix that, but we can certainly take action to make the search a little easier. Creative solutions can be very effective and inexpensive. Our customers who are our bosses deserve our best efforts.

In Summary

Unemployed Customers often use the library as a resource for finding new jobs. Libraries can help by featuring items useful to jobseekers, such as access to computers and word processing software, printers, reference items, and message boards. Computer usage time should be limited in order to accommodate as many customers as possible. Host workshops featuring speakers who offer advice on job-seeking tips, resume writing and interview skills. Unemployment can be a traumatic experience. Offer references to counseling services and aid agencies that help people who are struggling between jobs.

HOMELESS CUSTOMERS: LIVING IN THE SHADOWS OF SOCIETY

There's no place like home.

—Dorothy, in *The Wizard of Oz*

If you are working in a public library, you probably encounter Homeless People loitering in your facility from time to time. There's nothing wrong with hanging out at the library, meeting friends, and socializing. Lots of people do that, and the Homeless certainly have that right, too; but it's not the same as creating a nuisance, sleeping, and disturbing other customers. This certainly isn't unique to big cities; small communities aren't immune to the effects of homelessness. In this book as we talk about problem library customers, we should clarify that Homeless Folks aren't problem customers so much as customers with problems, big problems. Something in their lives changed so dramatically, it forced them into the streets with what appears to be nowhere to turn.

These people have run out of options. Perhaps they've already worn out their welcome, couch surfing with family or friends, or they don't have a support network in their lives they can turn to. For the Homeless who are unable to secure a place to live on their own, a library represents a comfortable and civilized place to escape the streets. It's clean, quiet and safe. It has restrooms and reasonably comfortable furniture. It's warm and dry in the winter, and cool in the summer. It provides all the comforts of home.

While it may be difficult to confront people whom you suspect are squatters in the library, your facility is not equipped to be someone's home, and should not be treated as such. You have a duty to maintain the integrity and the reputation of your library, which means taking decisive action to curtail this type of activity.

It's encouraging to know there are things you can do to help. The resources listed at the end of this section contain a wealth of information, specific to your state, with suggestions on how to help these displaced individuals. Your community may have organizations that offer shelter and assistance to, for example, battered women, young mothers with children or teenage runaways escaping their abusers. A little research and a few phone calls will quickly assemble a sizable emergency assistance contact file to help you resolve situations like these.

Meanwhile, consider how the Homeless and vagrants affect your library. Part of a library's appeal is the condition of the furniture, and carpeting. No one wants to use a chair or study carrel that's soiled, smelly or dirty. The same goes for stained, grimy carpet. The staff has better things to do than follow odors around and spritz Lysol all day. The restrooms are an even greater concern. They're a ready source of soap, water and paper towels, perfect for impromptu bathing. While no one would begrudge an individual the use of a restroom, sink-bathing pushes the limits of hospitality. This poses more sanitary problems and creates uncomfortable situations for other customers who enter the restrooms. This scenario is particularly disturbing if it involves children.

It's human nature for people to fear what they don't understand. The presence of a Homeless Person may be troubling to many customers who don't know if that person can be trusted or might even be dangerous. It doesn't help that Homeless People usually have understandable hygiene issues, which make them even more unattractive. The condition of homelessness instills dread, reminding us all how uncertain life can be and how "There, but for the grace of God, go I." No one aspires to become Homeless.

Alcoholism and drug addiction are common causes of homelessness. For these individuals, it's likely you will find them under the influence while in your library. A cautious approach is warranted should they become angry or belligerent when you confront them. Depending on their condition, their behavior could become threatening or even violent. Don't hesitate to contact the authorities if you feel the need for police assistance, even for that initial contact. Your community may have laws prohibiting public intoxication, in which case calling the police is your only option. (Appendix A)

Foreclosures and long-term unemployment also result in homelessness. In many foreclosures, the people left homeless aren't the property owners but their renters who are blindsided with the news they have to pack up and move out. Because many in this group are better equipped to recover, their homelessness may not be as long term but just as troublesome. Making available the library's job assistance resources for unemployed customers will certainly benefit individuals in search of work. Your database of emergency assistance contacts should include resources for temporary housing.

People who suffer from mental illness or post-traumatic stress disorder may also experience homelessness, compounded by their inability to access needed medication. This type of customer is described in the section on the Mentally Ill Customer. Their inability to function and communicate normally makes them particularly vulnerable. Attempting to help them can be difficult when they are confused or delusional and resist your offer to help, even though they desperately need it. For these individuals, contact the police for assistance in transporting them to the appropriate medical facility.

Some Homeless Individuals may resort to panhandling and approach library customers for money, cigarettes, etc. Be aware that this activity, like vagrancy, may be prohibited in your community. It's important to discourage this behavior because failing to do so will only invite more of the same. Left unchecked, it can discourage customers from using your library, particularly people with children. It's easier for them simply to find a different library with a more nurturing atmosphere than to frequent one where they and their children are confronted and badgered.

The problem is, these people are probably unknown to you. Are they dangerous? Are they unstable? Are they just down-on-their-luck, victims of economic circumstances?

Your library policies should work in concert with local laws to define unwanted loitering, public intoxication, indecent exposure, etc. Don't forget to include language regarding the inappropriate use of the restrooms or monopolizing library furnishings for sleeping. Any activity that disrupts library services and disturbs other customers should be prohibited. These policies should apply to all library users and should be enforced equally.

Have a flyer on hand listing homeless shelters, food kitchens, social services, etc. Need some help getting your emergency assistance contact list started? We've provided a few national sources of aid for the Homeless, all available online. Check for the resources available in your state or specific to your location, and don't forget to contact your local humanitarian organizations, food banks, and churches.

- United States Interagency Council on Homelessness (www.usich.gov)
- U.S. Department of Housing and Urban Development, Homelessness Resource Exchange (http://homeless.samhsa.gov/channel/us-department-of-housing-and-urban-development-homelessness-resource-exchange-hudhre-496.aspx)
- U.S. Department of Health and Human Services (www.hhs.gov/homeless)
- National Resource Directory (www.nrd.gov/homeless_assistance)
- Homeless Assistance: National Resource Directory

In Summary

During recessionary times and downswings in the economy, the number of Homeless Customers in libraries will grow. The library is a comfortable place, offering shelter from the elements. Unless they are panhandling or sleeping in the library (which should be addressed in your library's behavior policy), the Homeless should be treated with the same courtesy and respect as any other library patron. Some of those in the homeless community who have mental and emotional issues may need referrals to other agencies.

MENTALLY ILL CUSTOMERS: SOCIETY'S MOST MISUNDERSTOOD

It's so horrible to see your own confusion and understand it.
—Ingmar Bergman, *Through a Glass Darkly,* 1961

The first thing Robin tells you when she introduces herself is that she has extreme Obsessive-Compulsive Disorder (OCD). Not every library customer with mental and/or emotional issues will give you a heads-up. In Robin's case, you soon discover that, in addition to the OCD, she goes off like a rocket fueled by fury if you point at the computer screen, a book on the shelf, anything. We've learned to literally sit on our hands when she's at the reference desk. Instead of pointing at a list of books, we'll turn the monitor screen toward her and say, "I think number four would be a good choice for you." When we walk her to the stacks, we tell her, "If you check the fifth shelf down on the second stack from the right, you'll see a red book in the middle." If you don't point, Robin can be a delightful person, but the Ms. Hyde that emerges if you do point is quite a force to be reckoned with.

Ask any librarian and you're likely to learn that every library has its own cast of unique characters; but how do you tell the difference between the harmless eccentrics and people with true psychological disorders? The distinction between unusual and abnormal behavior can be hard to discern, particularly when so many symptoms of mental illness aren't always visible. Obviously, library staff members aren't going to recognize all the nuances of mental illness. We're not suggesting you need to make a study of it, but staff should know how to react correctly if a situation arises, to avoid any harm to the Mentally Ill Person, or other customers. In Robin's case, the solution is to avoid pointing at anything.

According to NAMI, the National Alliance on Mental Illness, one in every four Americans is affected by mental illness every year. NAMI lists specific mental illnesses as (http://www.nami.org/Template.cfm?Section=By_Illness):

- Anxiety Disorders
- Autism Spectrum Disorders
- Attention-Deficit/Hyperactivity Disorder (ADD/ADHD)
- Bipolar Disorder
- Borderline Personality Disorder
- Depression
- Dissociative Disorders
- Dual Diagnosis: Substance Abuse and Mental Illness
- Eating Disorders
- Obsessive-Compulsive Disorder (OCD)
- Panic Disorder
- Posttraumatic Stress Disorder
- Schizoaffective Disorder
- Schizophrenia
- Seasonal Affective Disorder
- Tourette's Syndrome

Library staff will deal with people with mental illness, maybe on a daily basis. Staff needs to be concerned with the type of customers who fit the clinical profile of "psychologically abnormal." These people exhibit behaviors that are self-destructive and/or interfere with their ability to function in society, including your library. Customers who appear to harm themselves, have difficulty communicating, or are withdrawn or hyperactive, may fit this description. While there are medications available to treat these disorders, not all sufferers have access to them, and some discontinue taking their meds for a variety of reasons, allowing their symptoms to return.

The fact is, people who suffer from mental illness are often more of a threat to themselves than to others, but even the most innocent of abnormal behaviors can become harmful. For example, those who suffer from OCD become obsessed with cleanliness and organization, which compels them to engage in repetitive rituals. These are hardly threatening behaviors until they are taken to extremes, which people with OCD tend to do.

OCD causes sufferers to exhibit odd, repetitive motions they are unable to resist, even though they are fully aware of their actions. Counting, touching, or tapping objects, and an obsession with symmetry are hallmarks of this disorder. In fact, by giving in to these urges, the compulsion becomes even stronger, making them even harder to resist. People with this disorder also have irrational fears, which can include the fear they may harm someone or carry out some violent thought.

Not all symptoms appear as abnormal behaviors, and they're not always apparent. People suffering from paranoid schizophrenia, for example, may be withdrawn or exhibit inappropriate emotional responses with no other outside indication of their condition. They may be far more distressed than they appear. On the inside, they struggle with disordered thinking, become delusional and hallucinate, or find it difficult to communicate. We've had patrons come to the reference desk with their request written on a folded piece of paper "so the FBI and CIA can't hear us." One young man lay on the floor in front of one bookstack, had us retrieve a book from another stack, and hand it down to him "so the men who follow me won't know what I'm reading."

Those who experience clinical depression experience a variety of symptoms. They are troubled by acute feelings of sadness and hopelessness and are often morose, even on the verge of tears. They can have self-destructive thoughts and become highly irritable. Reading and concentrating can become difficult, and they may lose interest in personal hygiene.

Sufferers of manic depression, now known as bipolar disorder, have extreme mood swings, ranging from the heights of euphoria to the depths of depression. Sufferers in the manic phase often talk too fast and loud, racing from one thought to the next, and not always making sense. Their behavior can be hyperactive, grandiose, and even promiscuous. They may also become impatient to the point of aggression when displeased.

People with panic disorder and phobias are plagued by persistent and debilitating fears. Their attacks leave them cold, sweating, and shaking, often with difficulty breathing or feeling faint. Fear of the next attack, or of doing something embarrassing during an attack, heightens their anxiety, and they may turn to alcohol or drugs for relief.

These customers are vulnerable to not only their own urges and fears but also to the reactions of other customers who may mistake the inappropriate behaviors for rudeness, or make hasty and unfair judgments about them. However, any confrontation could trigger an unexpected outburst that could become extreme or even dangerous.

When it comes to managing tense situations involving Mentally Ill Customers, your options are limited. It's important to remember, these individuals may not be able to respond normally. Their strange behavior is not deliberate, but part of a disorder they cannot control. They are just as troubled by it as you are, if not more so.

When approaching someone exhibiting bizarre or inappropriate behavior, stay calm. Have another staff member on alert in case you need help. Greet the disturbed person in a quiet voice and ask if you can help. Don't argue with the person, no matter how preposterous their statements are. Listen to them carefully and politely, and don't interrupt or make jokes. Offer them alternatives. If they want to leave, don't try to detain them until the police or their caretaker arrives.

Staff at one library told us about Clara, a 50-something woman with the mental abilities of a 4-year old. She likes attention and comes to the library staff frequently for small requests, for example, to borrow a rubber band. She likes to "read" children's picture books although she is unable to read, but it has become necessary to keep her from staying in the children's room to read them. So, she'll sit in the adult area and make up own story to go along with the pictures, sometimes "reading" them out loud. Often, she gets overly excited, such as the day she was "reading" a story about a kitten and began meowing quite loudly. When she does such things, staff has to speak with her as they would with a child, and remind her that if she doesn't behave, she won't be allowed in the library. She can be sneaky, too, taking paper from the copier tray when no one is looking to draw pictures on, sometimes creating paper jams. Staff has had to tell her that's a "no-no" and instead, save scrap paper for her. When she gets angry, she can be spiteful. Once she ruined a $300 chair by urinating on it; so, staff had to tell her that she must sit only in wooden chairs in the future. On one occasion, she got angry at the staff, so she stopped up the sinks and the toilet, locked the door to the bathroom upon leaving, and let them run, causing quite a flood. For Clara, the worst punishment is the loss of her library privileges, so as long as staff reminds her frequently that she must behave or lose them, she controls herself fairly well.

It's likely that the Mentally Ill People who come into your library have been dealing with their disorders for some time. To them, a sudden attack or outburst is nothing new, and you are probably not the first to witness one; but with your help in handling the situations properly, it doesn't have to be a mortifying experience.

When you observe customers exhibiting what may be symptoms of mental illnesses, and again, these may be hard to discern, err on the side of caution. It's important to intervene early in these situations and take control to maintain order and head off any chance of confrontation. Respect their space and their dignity, even though, at the moment, their behavior may be far from dignified. Approach them carefully and with a great deal of patience and sensitivity to determine if they're in need of help. Try speaking in a calm, gentle voice that shows your concern, but be direct and honest. Never argue with them or correct them. They may not be thinking clearly, so let your voice and body language communicate that you care and want to help. Never judge their intelligence by their behavior. They are often brighter and far more aware than people realize.

If they are library customers, their contact information, including phone numbers, should be on file. Offer to contact a family member or friend for them, someone who knows their condition and can help. In our experience, family members or group home supervisors often leave their contact information and request to be notified when there is a problem. You might also contact their doctor if the information is available. Be sure your customer's personal items, such as purses or backpacks, among other loose items, remain with them and are not misplaced during the crisis. To the extent possible, protect their privacy to minimize the self-consciousness they are likely to feel.

Some Mentally Ill People struggle with the added complication of homelessness. A 2008 study by the National Resource and Training Center on Homelessness and Mental Illness, revealed that up to a quarter of single adult homeless people, usually males, suffer some form of mental illness. Without a home address, they're not library cardholders with contact information. Many have fallen out of contact with family and friends. They come to the library for shelter or a safe place to sit or sleep. Your community may have agencies or churches that provide help to the homeless, or you can check with other area libraries to see what resources they recommend and consider making a master list to distribute of places that offer assistance. Police and fire department crisis responders may also have contact information for shelters and other homeless services.

In Summary

It is hard to discern the harmless eccentrics from the seriously Mentally Ill Customer. Be alert to behaviors that may indicate there is a problem. Mentally Ill Customers may not react "normally" when approached. Use caution, but respect their space, intelligence, and possessions. Never argue or contradict them. Be prepared to contact help, family members, or other agencies if the need arises.

PARANOID PATRONS: SOMEONE'S OUT TO GET ME!

"Why are you so paranoid, Mulder?"
"Oh, I don't know. Maybe it's because I find it hard to trust anybody."
—Scully & Mulder, *The X-Files*, "Ascension"

Customer "X" who wouldn't tell us what his name was looked repeatedly from side-to-side and then behind him all the way to the reference desk. Even though he'd stopped walking, his 360 degree glances didn't stop. He handed the librarian a multifolded note. It was written in pencil, and the writing was shaky. Phrases, coherent and not, covered both sides of the page. He wrote another note as he stood there: "I can't talk. The FBI has implanted listening devices in my fillings." Then he left; and we never saw him again.

Another customer needed to do some research, but all of the materials he needed were on the bottom shelf. He said he couldn't sit on the floor to look at the books because "someone would arrest him." He was extremely upset, so we pulled the books he needed and put them on a book truck so he could study them while sitting in a chair in the corner, away from everyone.

Cherie, one of our regulars, won't leave the reference desk until the librarian deletes the history of her searches so no one can see them and use them against her. We weren't sure how harmful a question such as "What's the difference between Baroque and Rococo architecture?" could be, but we always comply with her request, and quickly. If anyone comes near the reference desk while she's there, she gets very agitated.

Sometimes Paranoid Customers have other serious problems. Ruby comes to the library frequently to conduct "research." She spends hours taking notes from reference books and then typing them on the library typewriter we keep for people who can't use a computer. She talks out loud as she writes or types, sometimes very loudly. We have been told that she was a schoolteacher in her home country, but has some mental issues and refuses to stay on her medication. Her family has given up trying, so they just let her roam, and roam she does, usually to the library. Sometimes, the teens in the library will harass her because they love to see her get angry, which she does easily and loudly, swearing in several languages. When she finishes her "research," she makes multiple photocopies and gives us one that she requests be put on file in the archives for future use by other researchers. Fortunately, she doesn't remember well, so we thank her for her contribution and then place it in "File 13." She goes to every City Council meeting and, during the "comments from the public" portion, complains about being persecuted in the library. Council knows her well, so they don't hold her comments against the library. Even though she's difficult and sometimes cantankerous, we realize that it's our duty as library staff to keep others from bullying her and allow her to do her "research."

Paranoia in your customers isn't something that staff can "pooh-pooh" or tell the troubled person they're in no danger; there's nobody after them. Don't argue with the Paranoid Person. It will upset them, and soon, you'll be on the list of those persecuting them.

In Summary

To the Paranoid Person, their enemies are real. They believe the FBI will arrest them for sitting on the floor, or secret agents will steal their research. Staff needs to avoid arguing with them and protect them from any bullies who have noted their abnormal behaviors. Sometimes, Paranoid People are dangerous, so don't hesitate to call the police if you feel the person you're dealing with has the potential to hurt someone.

PART VI

"Just the Facts, Ma'am": When Patrons Break the Law

DOODLERS AND OTHER BOOK DEFACERS: YOUR BOOK IS MY CANVAS

> If you rip, tear, shred, bend, fold, deface, disfigure, smear, smudge, throw, drop, or in any other manner damage, mistreat, or show lack of respect towards this book, the consequences will be as awful as it is within my power to make them.
>
> —J.K. Rowling

A father came up to our circulation desk. He was furious. His child had used a Magic Marker to leave his artwork and other scribbles on almost every page in one of our brand new picture books. A sharp-eyed staff member discovered the drawings before checking in the book, and the man had received a bill for a replacement. "This is a children's book!" he yelled. "You should expect them to be written in!"

Well, we don't.

Library books are subjected to a host of abuses. They are often marked up. We've found highlighting, underlining, and even editorializing in the margins. One patron left comments throughout the margins of a book written by a well-known political pundit: "This isn't true!" "This is a lie!" "Can you believe this guy?" She had a right to disagree with the author, but she didn't have a right to share those opinions by defacing the library's book.

We had quite a few books damaged when a teacher at a nearby, low-income school insisted her students submit colored pictures with their essays. We discovered this when a couple of children from her class sat on the floor between the stacks ripping out pages for their assignment. We contacted the teacher and explained the situation, but the next year, she gave the same requirement for student essays. It was no surprise that once again, our books were defaced.

Books are sometimes used for telephone messages when no other paper is available. Lazy readers fold down the corners of pages to remind them where they've stopped reading for the day. Sloppy eaters leave food and drink stains on library books.

Writings, drawings, tears, coffee and food stains, all of these things damage library books and contribute to the diminished quality of the collection. Unfortunately, the expense of replacing these books sometimes makes it necessary to keep damaged titles in circulation longer, despite their poor condition. Of course, there are always publication realities to consider. A damaged out-of-print title is more likely to be kept in the collection than one that can be readily replaced.

The most effective way to minimize damage and capture at least part of the replacement fee is to train your circulation staff to look for damage as they check in library materials. If you are understaffed, as so many of us are, cleaning books and making simple repairs is a great job for volunteers. Once a book, magazine, or DVD is checked in, there's usually no way to find out which library customer had it last. The one caveat is that the person who last checked out an item might not be the one who defaced it. Books and other library materials with food-encrusted covers, bent pages, and other messiness, should be set aside at check-in for repair, cleaning, or both. No one wants to take a filthy book home, and in a way, letting dirty items circulate shows a lack of respect for your customers as well as a lack of pride in your collection.

In Summary

Damaged and soiled books devalue your library collection and make your items less than desirable to check out. It is important to do a quick inspection of items as they are checked in so the person responsible for any damages can pay whatever replacement and processing fees are necessary. Cleaning dirty book covers and doing simple repairs are good tasks for volunteers. Your customers should never have to take home books or other library materials that are filthy and torn.

VANDALS: THIS IS WHY WE CAN'T HAVE NICE THINGS

Art is the symbol of the two noblest human efforts: to construct and to refrain from destruction
—Evelyn Waugh

What is it about public places that makes people think it is acceptable to do things they'd never do anywhere else? What are they thinking? People don't carve their initials into the dining room table at home. So why do it to a study table at the library? We doubt anyone stuffs paper towels into the bathroom sink at home and then runs off, letting water overflow onto the floor, or worse, sets the towels on fire. Yet it seems that not a week goes by without some sort of restroom catastrophe at the library. So what do you do?

The fact is, public places, like libraries, are popular targets for Vandals because such places are high profile and busy, where the Vandal's daring antics are likely to gain the most attention with the least chance of being caught. The object is to inflict damage and get away with it. Much vandalism is performed by teens, emboldened by such factors as alcohol, peer pressure, gang initiation, and revenge or spite. Over the years we've seen it all: graffiti, broken windows, trashed restrooms, damaged library materials, equipment tampering, tripped alarms and fires, and that's just on the inside! The building's exterior and the parking lot are just as vulnerable.

Video security systems are great for libraries that can afford them and can justify the expense. Vandals who know they're being watched are more likely to find other targets, rather than risk being caught. The cost savings realized from the reduction in vandalism helps to offset at least part of the system's maintenance cost. However, for libraries that are operated on shoestring budgets, the vigilance of staff is the best defense.

People are creatures of habit. We generally park in the same area at the grocery store and use the same entrance nearly every time. We sit in our usual row or section at church and we tend to return repeatedly to our favorite spot in the library. Over time, observant staff gets a feel for the behavior patterns of the regulars, and even the not-so-regulars. So when the suspected table carvers return to their favorite spots, if for no other reason than to see if their handiwork is still there, making your presence known is a great starting point. You may never be able to connect them directly to the damage, but the knowledge that you're suspicious and watching has an effect similar to video security.

It helps to keep Vandal-prone areas and items, such as restrooms and valuable equipment, within the line of sight of the circulation and reference desks. It's impossible to monitor them constantly and serve customers at the same time. Vandals count on this distraction to do their thing. Fortunately for us, they often exhibit telltale behavior that gives them away. Restlessness, huddled laughter, or wandering about watching the desks with no apparent purpose, are often indications of potential Vandals. Of course, not everyone who exhibits these behaviors is necessarily a Vandal. Let common sense and your gut feelings guide you. Once you've narrowed the scope of people to keep an eye on, it makes the task more manageable. Alerting other staff to the suspicious individuals increases your odds of catching or deterring them.

Vandalism of library materials is the most difficult to prevent. Anyone can toss an open can of soda, a balloon full of urine, or even burning rags into the book drop after hours. Keeping the area around the book drop well lighted is a simple deterrent, although not foolproof. We empty the book drop as the last order of business at closing time, which helps to minimize damage, should vandalism occur during the night.

Defacing items in the stacks or study carrels is probably the most common form of library vandalism. Unfortunately, when the perpetrators see you coming before you see them, it makes it nearly impossible to catch them in action. Still, strolling through the stacks and study areas from time to time, making your presence known, is often enough to spoil their fun. If you suspect mischief, offer to reshelve the items they're finished with so other customers can use them.

Each library's vandalism experience is different. The best remedies are born of common sense and an observant staff. People who are suspected of possible vandalism are still just library customers, albeit persons of interest, until they're caught. When they enter the library, acknowledge their presence with direct and deliberate recognition, and keep them within sight. This amount of VIP attention is inconvenient for Vandals who prefer to go unnoticed. Your sudden interest may make your library more trouble than it's worth. In all situations, maintain your professionalism.

Obviously, a few scratches on the furniture or some defaced books aren't necessarily grounds for police action unless they are hateful, gang related, or threatening in nature. Serious, criminal damage inside the library is another matter. For this, notify the authorities as soon as it is discovered, and keep the other customers away from the affected area until it can be investigated. Document the incidents, no matter how minor, in as much detail as possible for possible reference later. (See Appendix A.)

Some states have library vandalism laws. This is the case with Massachusetts and California (Appendix I). In 1990, the Massachusetts law was amended to extend the punishment of Vandals from six months to "not more than two years," and the fine range increased to $100 to $1,000, or both.

Damage to the outside of the building or fixtures will require not only police action, but also a visit from the Risk Manager, who may need to pursue an insurance claim. Damages done to vehicles in the parking lot are individual matters for the owners to resolve. However, posting signs to alert customers to the danger helps them to be more cautious and aware, something vandals find inconvenient.

Minor and criminal vandalism each require a different level of response, and should be covered in your policy manual. Seek the assistance of the police department in developing this policy, and be sure to include the roles of staff so everyone understands the safety concerns and knows what *not* to do. Include a call list of the people to notify and samples of the required forms for easy reference.

In Summary

Public places, like libraries, are frequent targets for Vandals who are most often teens emboldened by some outside influence like peer pressure, gang initiation, alcohol and other motivators. Common types of vandalism include graffiti, broken windows, trashed restrooms, damaged library materials, equipment tampering, tripped alarms and fires. A watchful, informed staff is an effective deterrent. Suspicious behavior often precedes acts of vandalism. Stroll through the stacks and study areas occasionally to make your presence known. If possible, restrooms and expensive equipment should be visible to the circulation or reference desks. Vandals are less likely to act if they know someone is watching. Minimize vandalism to book drops by keeping them well lighted, and emptying them at the end of the day. Shelve often-defaced items behind the desk to protect them between checkouts. Seek police input in developing a vandalism policy. Document all incidents of vandalism, no matter how minor, and promptly report any that qualify as criminal activity.

HACKERS AND OTHER COMPUTER TAMPERERS: TAKE MY DATA. PLEASE

There is no such thing as a secure network.

—Stephen Hunter, IT Administrator

Not all people who access your system from their homes or come in the library to use your computers have library business on their minds. They might have different plans. In fact, they might be Hackers.

In the book *Takedown: The Pursuit and Capture of Kevin Mitnick, America's Most Wanted Computer Outlaw By the Man Who Did It* (1996), the question is asked: "Are hackers a threat?" Mitnick's answer is general, and could apply to anything: "The degree of threat presented by any conduct, whether legal or illegal, depends on the actions and intent of the individual and the harm they cause."

Mitnick observed in an article in *The Guardian*, "Should we fear hackers? Intention is at the heart of this discussion" (February 22, 2000). Intention defines the two major types of Hackers: the amateurs and the criminal professionals. Basically, amateur Hackers break into computer systems just to see if they can. It gives them a sense of superiority and power. These Hackers prefer big targets with large scopes of influence. In fact, the bigger and more high-profile the target, the better. Amateur Hackers are like the Rebels. They not only feel that rules don't apply to them, but also show their disdain for these rules through their actions. They show off their prowess by finding a flaw in the operating system and exploiting that flaw. Still, Hackers can cause problems. For example, if justified, they might target an institution with a denial of service attack. The amateur Hacker is not always stealthy; they want you to see their accomplishments. Not so for the professional criminal Hacker.

The intentions of the professional criminal Hackers are different than those of the amateur Hackers. The professional criminal Hackers steal data to add to their own fortunes. They develop password "file crackers" that can decrypt password patterns. They collect these passwords, along with other personal data, so they can retrieve your customers' personal, and eventually, financial information. Professional criminal Hackers look for access to credit card numbers, Social Security numbers, birthdates, anything that can provide enough information for them to eventually link to bank accounts.

Professional criminal Hackers might use a "brute force" approach and send the system hundreds of thousands of passwords. Many people use basic passwords: pass1234, password, library, 2468, and so on. These are easily hacked. Longer passwords with mixed symbols, for example, cove7do62or#mt!2?, are more secure. Another option is to use computer-generated passwords. These are safer, too, but they're long, odd, and hard to remember. This makes them unpopular with end users.

Many organizations consider hacking prevention part of the cost of doing business. In a way, it is. They hire an information technology (IT) specialist who's knowledgeable about computer security. This person has to be trustworthy, because he or she controls access to the system and determines which users have read-only access, and which have read/write access. Organizations pay to install security on their router or buy a firewall as a separate utility. The IT specialist decides what specific firewall ports are open to end users, and which aren't.

According to one of our sources, an anonymous amateur Hacker, libraries that typically allow remote access to their users need to be watchful. Permissions should be kept to a minimum, and customers need to have read-only access. Administrative accounts should have limited access, and they need to be guarded "zealously."

The best security for administrative accounts is to not allow remote access changes to the system. The ability to make changes while physically away from the system provides an opportunity for Hackers to turn a "bot" loose to find the login port. A bot, short for "robot," is a computer program that acts like a human user when interacting with other programs. After the bot locates the login port, Hackers install another bot to discover the actual system passwords. Fortunately, there are tools that detect bot attacks, and these should be in place to protect your system.

You, as the manager, are expected to ensure patron data such as name, address, phone number, and credit card used to pay fines are secure. If you have in-house control of your library computer system, hire an excellent IT administrator, and communicate with that person at least daily to keep updated on the status of the system.

If you are part of a city or county network, get to know the IT staff. Be sure to show appreciation when they do something for the library. There will be times you need to go to them with computer problems, so you should cultivate a good relationship with them. However, no matter who controls the computer system, backups need to be current, and threat and damage assessment should be ongoing.

Computer science pioneer Ken Thompson wrote, "It is only the inadequacy of the criminal code that saves the hacker from very serious prosecution" (*Hackers: Crime and the Digital Sublime*, p. 123). Ironically though, the best advice you'll receive about computer security might very well be from a Hacker.

In Summary

The two types of Hackers are the amateur and the professional criminal. Regardless of the Hacker's reason for breaking into your computer system, you need to have safeguards in place to protect your system and data. The first line of defense is an excellent, trustworthy IT administrator. The second is a firewall, as well as other utilities, if necessary. After all, you, as manager, are ultimately responsible for the safety and security of your computer system.

THIEVES: PEOPLE WHO WEED YOUR COLLECTION FOR YOU

The number one rule of thieves is that nothing is too small to steal.

—Jimmy Breslin

Ideally, the only Thieves in the library should be Ali Baba and his band of forty. Unfortunately, as we all know, this isn't the case in the real world. No one "type" of person steals from your library, making him or her very difficult to identify. Thieves cover the whole range of ages, ethnicities, sexes, and yes, religions. They are your customers, volunteers, and even staff members. Occasionally, the Thief is someone who has never been to your library before and, like the item they steal, will never show up again.

So what motivates these people to deplete your library of its hard-earned collection?

1. The economy. As people lose their jobs and their homes, some will turn to theft to supplement their family budgets. Your CDs and DVDs are easily sold at swap meets. They can also be sold to unscrupulous pawnshop owners.
2. Drug addictions. To support their habit, drug users will sell your entertainment media and anything else that isn't nailed down.
3. Examinations. Many of the people who need to pass a test to get into college, join the armed services, or retain a certification help themselves to your library's copy of the appropriate study guide. These study guides include the GED, SAT, ACT, GRE, and ASVAB, as well as examinations for nurses, police officers, mail carriers, EMTs, and firefighters.
4. Obsession with celebrities and pop icons. Fans of popular sports figures, rock stars, and even famous criminals will add your library's books about such celebrities as Selena and John Lennon to their own collections.
5. Censorship. Some library theft is due to people who think certain types of books don't belong in libraries, and that other people have no business reading them. In one library, we discovered that in every branch, all copies of a particular book that told about secret rites of a certain religion were checked out. Oddly enough, they were all "lost" by the people who checked them out. These customers cheerfully paid for their "lost" copies, but theft is theft, and more was stolen than just the books themselves. The materials and hours of staff time that went into those books were basically wasted. And time, as the saying goes, "is money."
6. Secrecy. We found that books exposing the secrets about certain organizations, especially "secret societies," were often stolen. Once again, the people "losing" their copies paid lost fees. Maybe that eased their consciences. Who knows?
7. Anger with the library or someone who works there. We have had books that were not only stolen, but also destroyed and then returned to the library in battered condition.
8. Kleptomania. Some people can't help stealing things. It's an illness.
9. Bibliophilia. Bibliophiles love books, and sometimes, this leads to theft. For example, your library might have a book they really want, but can't afford to purchase. Extreme bibliophiles love books so much that they steal the volumes to protect them. These individuals can't stand the idea of rare, expensive books being manhandled by the public. So they take these books to their homes, where they feel they're safer. Sometimes, these bibliophiles are staff and volunteers who can easily bypass the system and remove the items from the library undetected.
10. Obsession with the paranormal. No doubt you've noticed how fast your books about the paranormal disappear. If books are about dreams, Nostradamus, end-world predictions (if you're reading this, you know Nostradamus' end-of-world prediction didn't happen), Mayan calendars, the occult, palmistry, UFOs, or ESP, they usually have very short shelf-lives in the library.
11. School deadlines. Students at deadline can be some of our most frantic customers. Especially targeted for theft are books with pictures they can use for their reports.

12. Pregnancy. Some parents-to-be, especially young ones, have a sudden need for information. Why buy expensive books on pregnancy, childbirth, and baby names, when the library collection has all of these, and they're ripe for the picking?
13. Need for specific information. Car repair books are a good example of this. People who steal car repair manuals don't have to worry about paying library fines or damages on grease-stained books when they're returned after being properly borrowed. Plus, they'll always have their stolen manuals as references for making future repairs.
14. Reasons where your guess is as good as ours. A few years ago, a small college library did an inventory of their collection. The subject area with the most stolen items was "Morals and Ethics." Maybe if the Thieves had read the books first, the thefts wouldn't have happened!

How do people steal your library items? Often, Thieves go to the restroom to slip the books, CDs, DVDs, and other items into backpacks, purses, underclothing, or even into diaper bags. Sometimes, a popular CD or DVD is removed from its library box and switched for another carried by the Thief. An experienced Thief knows about security strips and where they're located, and will remove them before leaving the library. In libraries with outdoor patios, a Thief can throw whatever is stolen over a fence or wall to a friend, or retrieve it himself later. Methods of theft are only as limited as a Thief's imagination.

Every little bit hurts. With library theft, we tend to think in terms of larger or more expensive items. Nevertheless, when you think about it, the loss of many small items, even copies of magazines and journals, can do just as much damage to your budget when they need to be replaced repeatedly because someone has stolen them from your library. Small costs amount to big dollars. When you figure the cost of these items you also need to estimate what it costs to process them in staff time, as well as materials as the replacements go from acquisitions to receiving to cataloging to processing to shelving. These are all very real costs.

A wide spectrum of philosophies about library theft exist. At one end are librarians who feel that no matter what, a few people will steal from them but most of their customers are good people who wouldn't dream of doing such a thing. They see no need to spend what little money they have on expensive and intrusive security systems. To them, a few stolen items are just part of doing business. At the other end of the spectrum are libraries with security systems, security guards, cameras, and so on. While these measures might discourage thefts, they can't eliminate it entirely. You need to determine which position your library will take.

Both approaches have pros and cons. The libraries with lax security may be overlooking the REAL cost of thefts. A great deal of labor is involved in getting a book from the publishers to the library shelf. If the book isn't out of print, and with the tax laws, this happens at lightning speed, staff needs to modify the previous catalog record, re-order the title, add it to the holdings, and process the replacement. When books or other library materials are stolen, supplies are stolen, too: barcodes, security strips, laminate, re-enforcement tape.

The maximum-security libraries train their staff to be alert to theft but sometimes forget the part about using tact, finesse, and courtesy. They may have overzealous staff who are bad for the library's image, and may, in fact, set it up for a lawsuit. They may embarrass innocent patrons. They do everything but strip search customers who set off the antitheft alarms.

One of our library customers, Irene, who moved to our town from another state, told us a horror story about her experience with library security. She has to use a walker, and she has a basket in the front to carry her things. Unfortunately, there's something about her walker that sets off certain library security systems. At her former library, even though the alarm sounded every time she went through the security gate, circulation staff would stop her and make her return to the desk, where they would empty everything from the basket, including her purse, onto the counter. Without fail, they would loudly comment about what they were doing. Even though Irene was mortified, she was on a fixed income that forced her to use this nearby library for books and tapes. Security measures should never embarrass the innocent.

Libraries need to find a happy medium, instructing their staff to be tactful and use common sense. Even the staunchest security person should remember two words: "False alarm."

A security system is an effective theft prevention device that any library with a theft problem or potential future problem should consider. Bear in mind, no security system is 100% effective; some Thieves will always find a way to defeat it. However, a good system will help keep the basically honest person honest.

Security systems are expensive, both to purchase and to maintain. Sometimes your library facility has to be modified to accommodate it. More costs go beyond installation. In addition to targeting your existing collection, it's necessary to purchase a security strip to place in each new book, periodical, or piece of media. Our library saved money here by joining a consortium. Staff time spent inserting or adhering the strip will also increase labor costs and processing time. You need to weigh these additional expenses against the cost of replacing stolen items, keeping mind that some items may be irreplaceable.

Be sure you have a balanced security policy. If it's too strict, you might accuse innocent people. If it's too lax, your library will be known as an easy mark, and materials will disappear at an increased rate. Have library security procedures in place before incidents occur, and make sure everyone on staff deals with such issues as customers setting off alarms in a calm, fair, and uniform manner. Consider the safety of staff and patrons, loss prevention, and liability issues when writing your policies and procedures. Always be sure they fall within the constraints of the law and don't violate anyone's rights. For the protection of both you and your library, your governing body's legal department should review all policies and procedures before they go into effect.

Other types of theft in the library don't involve your collection. Patron belongings, such as purses, wallets, laptops, notebooks, and cell phones, are also the targets of Thieves. Be aware of situations that invite theft, such as customers leaving their belongings on a table or chair while they browse the stacks. Of course, this is easier to do if you don't spend your shifts glued to your chair! Make your presence known. It's harder for Thieves to steal something if they know that staff might be watching, or could show up any moment.

Display your high-risk collections in secure or visible locations near your public service desks, not in isolated corners or back of the library. Shelf read areas containing these items on a regular basis. During processing, be sure that all materials are clearly and permanently marked with your library's name. This makes them harder to pawn.

Sometimes, vandalism accompanies the theft, particularly after hours. Our library once had a coin collection stolen from a glass display case. The Thieves threw a concrete-weighted ash can through our sliding glass door. When we discovered the break-in the next morning, we had to submit papers to our risk management department for the replacement costs of the door, the glass case, and the coin collection itself.

Thefts occurred during the construction of our main library. Every phone in the building was stolen, and then thrown into a ravine when the Thieves discovered they didn't work without the central system. New books were taken from book trucks, where they'd been stored while the shelving was being installed.

It's important for your collection development policy to address recurring thefts. Seriously, how many times does a specific title have to be stolen before you stop buying replacements? Do you keep replacing, or just stop stocking it? Be sure to involve staff when you write this policy. This will help to gain staff buy-in as well as make them aware of the true cost of a stolen book or piece of media.

You also need to factor in thefts in your materials replacement budget. Once this money runs out, do you reallocate money from another fund, or call a halt to replacements until the next fiscal year? Library funding allocations should be carefully examined each year to ensure appropriation is distributed correctly.

You can network with colleagues in the book and media business to learn how to prevent theft of certain titles. Ask local bookstore staff which items are being stolen from their inventories. Those titles are likely to be targeted at your library, too. Look for patterns of theft in your library. One way to do this is to track your interlibrary loan requests.

A Thief may hit more than one library. Let other librarians know about your theft patterns, and ask about theirs. Don't forget the pawnshops. That's where your stolen articles might very well land. Meet with owners of pawnshops and used bookstores. Ask them to let you know if items identified as belonging to your library show up at their businesses. We had one pawnshop owner who was especially diligent, and even donated CDs or DVDs for the library collection when we stopped by to retrieve our stolen materials.

Library theft might be covered in your state and local laws, too. Use this to add teeth to your policy. An example of this is Oklahoma's (Appendix J).

Library theft affects your collection, your budget, your customers, and your staff. It's important to prevent it in a manner that doesn't offend innocent patrons. After all, librarians are entrusted with one of the most valuable assets in your community, and you need to do your best to protect it in a manner that doesn't penalize the majority of your customers.

In Summary

No one "type" of person steals library materials. Anyone can be a Thief, including your staff and volunteers. Thieves steal for a variety of reasons, and certain items are particularly vulnerable: CDs and DVDs, which can be sold for cash, study guides, celebrity items, controversial items, pregnancy books, materials that expose secrets, occult and paranormal items, and just about anything collectable. Some Thieves steal for retaliatory reasons, or just to see if they can get away with it. Library theft has a significant impact on the budget. The cost of replacing stolen items is often weighed against the cost of installing security systems, which aren't 100% reliable, either. Train staff to recognize theft in progress and how to react with tact and good sense, to avoid causing embarrassing scenes or false accusations. Often theft occurs in patterns, so other libraries and bookstores in the area may also be affected by the same Thief.

PART VII

Dangerous Patrons

RACISTS, HOMOPHOBES, AND OTHER BIGOTS: FUELED BY HATRED

We must learn to live together as brothers or perish together as fools.

—Martin Luther King Jr.

It doesn't take a genius to see the devastation that racism and other forms of hatred can cause. From Hitler's Holocaust, to the Ku Klux Klan's (KKK) murders and intimidation tactics, to genocide attempts in today's world, millions of people have suffered and died. According to the Spring 2013 issue of The Southern Poverty Law Center's *Intelligence Report* (149: pp. 43–44) in 2012, there were 1,007 active hate groups in the United States, all equipped to bully, harass, and even kill.

A subtler racism can be found just under the surface. You see it in ethnic jokes and seemingly off-the-cuff remarks. You see it in the too-long stares at people wearing ethnic clothing or eyebrows raised at couples who are mixed-race or same-sex. You see it in snide comments about library customers struggling to communicate in English.

No place in a library is appropriate for racism or other hate-fueled attitudes. Racism is the extreme opposite of what libraries stand for. From equal access to the Right to Read, libraries have maintained their status as "the people's university," places where all people feel free to come, regardless of race, religion, ethnicity, or lifestyle.

The position of the American Library Association (ALA) is clear on this issue:

. . . libraries are a microcosm of the larger society and play an important and unique role in the communities they serve; they must seek to provide an environment free of racism, where all are treated with respect and dignity.

(*ALA Policy Manual*, Combating Racism B.3.2)

Sometimes, racist groups use your library to further their nefarious causes. You might find yourself in the same position as the California library director who had to let a neo-Nazi group use the meeting room. Without a strong library policy stating that library meeting rooms are solely for the use of library or library-sponsored activities, your library might very well become a favorite meeting spot for hate groups.

Racist materials can be a major dilemma for librarians. How do you balance intellectual freedom with social responsibility? On the social responsibility side, proponents ask, "Isn't adding racist materials to a collection actually bringing racism into the library?" Then there is the intellectual freedom question: "Don't all points of view need to be represented in a balanced library collection?" The argument is an old one, but still continues to be unresolved.

You can be proactive in the fight against racism, prejudice, homophobia, and so on. For example, the Boulder, Colorado, Public Library "Reading to End Racism" project is part of their multicultural outreach program. They partnered with Boulder Valley Middle Schools, the Women's International League for Peace & Freedom, and the Boulder Valley School District Multi Ethnic Action Committee. Through this program, students are involved in a conversation about racism. They read books on a specially prepared reading list, relate their personal experiences, and explore ways to handle racism.

The New York Public Library facilitated the creation of "Turn It Up @ The Library, a Podcast Series on Racism and on Racist Slurs & Homophobia." This podcast, made by teens at the 125th Street Branch of The New York Public Library, is still available on the New York Public Library website.

The Ralph Ellison Library, part of the Metropolitan Library System of Oklahoma County, partnered with the YWCA and the Respect Diversity Foundation to present "Reading to End Racism," an evening of readings and hands-on activities focusing on tolerance and diversity. Nationally, "Reading to End Racism," which was developed in Boulder, Colorado, provides communities with "programs that help to eliminate racism through interactive personal and literary programs that educate and empower youth."

Writer Audre Lorde, a civil rights activist, said, "It is not our differences that divide us. It is our inability to recognize, accept, and celebrate those differences." Celebrating diversity is a powerful way for your library to combat haters. Book displays, cultural events, programs, speakers, posters, reading lists, discussion and book groups are all tools against racism and hatred.

As librarians, we are bound by professional standards as well as basic decency to fight prejudice and discrimination in our libraries. Since 1936, the ALA has taken a strong stand against racism. Carrying on this tradition today, ALA "believes that the struggle against racism, prejudice, stereotyping, and discrimination is a continuous effort and must extend throughout its membership" (*ALA Policy Manual*, Combating Prejudice, Stereotyping, and Discrimination, B.3.3).

In Summary

People shouldn't be afraid to come to your library because they're Muslim, Hispanic, or gay. Your library should be welcoming to everyone, regardless of race, ethnicity, religion, or lifestyle. Although you might not be able to stop racism, homophobia, and others on a grand scale, you most certainly can try to bring it to a screeching halt at the entrance of your library.

GANGS AND GRAFFITI: SIGNS OF TROUBLE

A team is where a boy can prove his courage on his own. A gang is where a coward goes to hide.

—Mickey Mantle

Our library, as well as the park in which it is located, was considered "neutral territory" by local Gangs for many years. Then one Gang decided to increase its territory, and another Gang protested. We became a place where graffiti started appearing everywhere. We were tagged inside. Pens, pencils, and permanent markers were used to make gang signs on study carrels, tables, chairs, and bathroom stalls. Tags were etched into the bathroom mirrors. We began to keep cans of graffiti remover as well as small amounts of paint to cover what we couldn't eradicate. Outside, our slump block walls were spray painted. One afternoon, a maintenance worker used acetone to remove the spray paint on one of our outside walls. Fumes filled the library, and we had to evacuate it. The constant vigilance and clean-up efforts became annoying, but when a staff member was mugged going into the library, it brought home the fact that Gangs could be dangerous, too.

One library reports continued problems with skateboard Gangs. Despite signage prohibiting skateboarding and loitering, groups of teens race through the building or wait for staff to leave so they can skateboard on the sidewalk and concrete driveway leading to the library. They have become quite insolent, and return, even after being sent away by security time after time. Recently, they threw a rock through a window to protest their eviction. Where there are skateboard Gangs, customers and staff alike need to be protected. Besides the potential danger, there are also liability issues. To address the problem, the library posted signs, trained security guards, and made sure staff at all desks had the phone number for the police at their fingertips.

In many large urban areas, gang activity is as common as bus fare. In fact, statistics of the Federal Bureau of Investigation estimate there are 33,000 Gangs with a combined affiliation of 1.4 million active members in the United States today. One of our libraries is located in an area affected by Gangs. In fact, some of our cardholders either have connections to Gangs or have siblings who are gang members. That's just the way it is.

As policy-abiding cardholders, they're our customers. They borrow, return, and participate in library programs. However, if they enter the library as gang members, their illegal and potentially violent activity makes them particularly unwelcome. Our staff is trained to watch for and recognize the types of hand signals used by the local Gangs. Signs flashed among members of the same Gang aren't necessarily dangerous, but it's impossible to know everyone's affiliations, or what their flashed signals are communicating. An exchange of signals could easily end in a library customer being victimized, or erupt into something more dangerous, affecting more customers.

For this reason, staff is instructed to notify the police any time potential gang activity is detected inside the library, no matter how subtle. Even if nothing illegal is happening, taking a proactive approach and requesting that a police officer stroll through the library is often enough to discourage gang members from hanging around if they're not conducting library business. Librarians who employ security personnel have an even greater advantage.

Where there are gang members, you'll also find graffiti and the various symbols they use to mark the gang's territory. Even though the library is among the friendliest, most hospitable places in the neighborhood, the walls of our buildings are occasionally tagged with spray-painted graffiti. The cryptic messages communicate meanings that only gang members and savvy antigang law enforcement recognize.

Graffiti, when left unreported, invites even more graffiti. What starts as a single tag soon mushrooms into a full-blown war of gang symbols. The sooner the first tag is removed, or painted over, the better. Both our staff and our many attentive customers are great about reporting graffiti as soon they discover it. However, because graffiti is vandalism, the police will want to see and investigate it before it is removed. Keep staff and customers away from the tagged area until the investigation is completed.

Removing spray paint from a decades-old wall can become quite expensive. We are fortunate that our community employs a graffiti removal expert who takes care of obliterating gang tags. Many large cities have hotlines and websites that people throughout the community can contact to report graffiti in their neighborhoods. If your location doesn't have these resources, look for commercial power sprayer, painting or sandblasting companies who provide this service, or check local service organizations who may remove it for free. The investigating officer may also be able to recommend other removal options. The key is to act quickly to keep the problem from escalating.

Some graffiti "artists" have no gang affiliation whatsoever. They mark walls, fences, and buildings with their clandestine handiwork, which is often quite creative. However, this form of graffiti is also vandalism, and it must be removed.

Teaching young people about the fallacy of gang involvement is an investment in their futures. Gangs count on impressionable young people to be the next generation of members and the temptation to join can be difficult to resist. Encourage young customers, through library workshops and events directed at their age groups to explore a variety of constructive pastimes that help them to make better choices and take pride in their community. Ask your local police department's gang enforcement and public information experts for advice on simple educational materials you can make available to your customers. For more information, we recommend these federal resources for downloadable publications:

National Gang Center (www.nationalgangcenter.gov)
Office of Juvenile Justice and Delinquency Prevention (www.ojjdp.gov/programs/antigang)

Use caution when dealing with gang activity and leave the heavy lifting to the authorities. Your responsibility is to protect your customers and ensure their safety. Consult your police department in the development of your antigang behavior policy to ensure all factors are considered, and that it references prevailing antigang laws and clear reporting responsibilities (Appendix A).

In Summary

Gang activity at the library should be reported to the police immediately, even if it seems insignificant at the time. Train staff to watch for and recognize gang hand signals. An exchange of signals could easily lead to a dangerous encounter. Take a proactive approach to discourage gang members from remaining at the library by requesting some form of police presence, even if only a walk-through. Report all incidents of graffiti and allow time for police investigation before removal. Work with local law enforcement to develop programs that teach young people options that will help them make better choices. Ask for advice on simple educational materials you can make available to your customers, and assistance in developing your library policy.

SUBSTANCE ABUSERS: YOUR ADDICTION AFFECTS US ALL

I'm very serious about no alcohol, no drugs. Life is too beautiful.

—Jim Carrey

One librarian recently posted on Facebook: "There was the druggie who came up to me today to ask a question and drooled all over the circ desk as he leaned over it. Yuck!" It's not always this easy to tell when people are under the influence of alcohol or drugs, but there's a good chance their behavior will give them away. We've all seen it, the belligerent, abusive outbursts of a drunk, or the irrational, erratic ramblings and posturing of a drug user. Their presence creates the type of environment most customers want to avoid, and parents will steer their children well clear of a place that tolerates this activity.

What are the odds you'll experience Substance Abusers in your library? The National Institute of Health estimates there are almost 18 million adults in the United States who have problems with alcohol or are alcoholic (www.nlm.nih.gov/medlineplus/alcoholism.html). In addition, prescription and over-the-counter drugs are becoming increasingly popular among Substance Abusers. A recent government survey of 12th graders in the United States indicates this age group has tried more prescription drugs than the typical street varieties like cocaine and methamphetamine. The survey also revealed that the use of marijuana is increasing among 12th graders while the perception of risk is decreasing, and nearly half admitted to consuming alcohol within the last 30 days. That's a lot to consider.

Librarians are not the intervention police. What people choose to drink, smoke, snort, sniff, inject, or pop throughout the day is their business, however, ill advised. But when their substance abuse interferes with library operations or in any way disturbs customers, it's time to take action. The library manager, with the authority to eject unwanted visitors, might be the one to engage these public Substance Abusers. However, never approach an abuser alone. Bear in mind that the abuser's reaction to the confrontation may be unpredictable. If the situation is bad or escalates into something dangerous, consider having the police take care of it, because, by then, it probably warrants an arrest anyway.

In one of our experiences, a man came into the library and lost consciousness in front of the circulation desk. The circulation supervisor didn't realize he'd been drinking. She thought he'd collapsed from a heart attack. When library manager knelt to administer CPR, it was obvious from the overwhelming odor of alcohol that he'd had too much to drink and had simply passed out. We managed to revive him but feared he'd leave the library and attempt to drive in his inebriated condition. Instead, we guided him to a chair where we waited with him for the police to arrive. Naturally, he wasn't happy about being detained and threatened to urinate on the circulation desk. Fortunately, the officers walked in before he was able to make good on his threat, and they escorted him out.

In this case, the man complied and stayed in the chair where we'd asked him to wait. However, if he had become combative and difficult to handle, detaining him could have created a serious hazard for staff and customers. Had that happened, we would have let him leave but then notified the police of his departure and direction of travel. You can't risk the safety of your staff and customers by trying to detain someone who doesn't want to be detained.

Of course, Substance Abusers can disrupt the library from the outside too. One day, a man outside the library, who we later learned had taken a large amount of cocaine, jumped from a picnic table onto the roof and yelled that he had a gun and intended to "blow everyone away." Hearing this, we immediately locked the library doors and called the police. The staff quickly directed customers to a windowless, inner hallway to await the authorities, while the man remained on top of the building, spouting threats. Anyone approaching or leaving the library would have been an easy target. When the police arrived, they found the man, still pacing on the roof, yelling that he was "Jesus Christ," and threatening to shoot as many people as he could. Thankfully, one of the officers was able to talk him down. As it turned out, the man was armed with a large knife, but he had no gun.

Most often, Substance Abusers who create nuisances in the library are best removed with firm words and the threat of police. The prospect of arrest generally does the trick. However, people exhibiting extreme impairment should not be approached alone. These people have lost the ability to think rationally. Their behavior may become dangerous when provoked. Staff needs to know how to react to these situations, and training from the police department is a good place to start. Understanding how drugs and alcohol affect people will prepare staff to anticipate the behaviors typical of abusers. While you're at it, consider developing a procedure for emergencies including a code word to indicate when it's time to call the police. Hopefully, you'll never need to use it, but like fire insurance, it's good to know it's there.

These are radical examples. However, an even greater threat may happen when you discover people are dealing drugs in your library. You have even more obvious dangers and you need to report this to the police immediately.

In Summary

Because of the high number of Substance Abusers in this country, at some point, you and your staff will probably have to deal with an unpleasant or even dangerous situation. If people under the influence won't leave the library when asked, if it's apparent they're a danger to customers and staff, or if they're dealing drugs, don't hesitate to call the police. Be sure to have a code word all staff members and volunteers know as the signal to notify authorities. Don't forget that when there is urine or vomit clean-up involved, use the same procedure as you would for hazardous waste materials. (See Appendix K.)

SEXUAL DEVIATES: FLASHERS, MOLESTERS, LECHERS, AND OTHER PERVERTS

We don't protect our young, and we tolerate predators of our own species.
—Andrew Vachss (child protection consultant, children's attorney, and crime-fiction novelist)

A library is an ideal environment for perverts and other sex offenders to do their thing. It's a perfect place to find children and women who are alone and distracted. The tall bookstacks prevent a clear line of vision, and there are lots of blind corners, nooks, and crannies. People are conditioned to be quiet in the library and not raise their voices, let alone yell, even if they feel threatened. Security is usually spotty and often nonexistent.

In our combined experience, we've had interactions with the full range of sexual predators. At the lower end are the people who interfiled pornographic materials with our magazines and a foot-fetishist who said, "I'm doing an academic study, and I need to see your feet." At **the** dangerous end of the spectrum is a teenage boy who pulled a little girl into a nearby restroom and had begun to undress her.

What library hasn't dealt with a flasher? Unfortunately, they are quite common in the library world. We've seen so many over the years that we're surprised when any amount of time passes without an incident. Nevertheless, staff is frustrated by their ongoing presence. One library staff member posted this on Facebook: "Today I really enjoyed my job. I watched lots of security footage to catch a sexual deviant, spent time with my favorite Officer to catch a sexual deviant, then had staff actually recognize a sexual deviant on digital footage. Now, if he comes back in, I will get him with my bullwhip and my steak knife . . ."

You can't always depend on the law being on your side, even when you're right. For example, Pete would masturbate in the periodicals area on a regular basis. Staff would call the police, who would promptly escort him out. One day the police had to arrest him three times, but Pete came back each time and continued doing his thing. After his third arrest that day, the city judge decided that Pete's civil rights had been violated. She gave him a permanent library pass, and issued copies for both the library manager and the chief of police. If there had been a different judge, or the library had in place an approved policy and procedure for handling repetitive inappropriate behavior, Pete might have landed behind bars, or, at the very least, been given a restraining order to keep him out of the library. Here's the problem and the reason men like Pete get away with what they do. In our experience, the people, mostly women, who are targeted by these Sexual Deviates, are too embarrassed by the situation to report it and, often, we find out about these encounters after the fact from a third party. This was the case when a man actually ejaculated on one of our patrons while she knelt on the floor looking at gardening books with her teenage daughter. The woman, who was the wife of a prominent citizen, left without saying a word. Later, after she told her husband about the incident, he stormed into the library, ready to beat up everyone in the place for letting this happen. Of course, this was the first we'd heard of it. The perpetrator got away because his victim was too mortified to yell or immediately report what he'd done to her.

Emotionally charged or inappropriate responses to perverts can be dangerous. Your best defense is in excellent staff training and cooperation with the police department. First, ask the police to conduct a safe environment study of the library. They'll point out likely places for criminal encounters and advise you of corrective measures to make your library safer for staff and patrons. Invite the police to speak to your staff about security, and have them review your behavior policy. Make sure your staff is familiar with this policy (Appendix B) and post copies of it in both the staff and public areas.

See to it that every staff member knows what information the police will need when they are called about an incident at the library (Appendix A). Role-play proper responses. Tell your staff that if

From *Crash Course in Dealing with Difficult Library Customers* by Shelley E. Mosley, Dennis C. Tucker, and Sandra Van Winkle. Santa Barbara, CA: Libraries Unlimited. Copyright © 2014.

an incident does occur, it's okay to scream and yell for help; in fact, have them practice yelling. This will make them feel more comfortable about screaming should the need arise, plus it's fun and a great stress releaser. We suggest you do this while the library is closed to avoid creating a panic among the customers.

Some ways to spot Deviates before they strike include: watch for out-of-the-ordinary behavior or things that don't add up. This includes adults by themselves who hang around the children's or youth department or someone who comes in and stalks or just stares at certain customers or staff. As we've recommended before, don't stay at your desk all the time. Wander around occasionally to patrol the stacks. You can proactively help library customers along the way and see what's going on at the same time.

When someone engages in illegal activity:

- Call 911 immediately (Appendix A).
- Be able to give a detailed description.

    1. Gender
    2. Race
    3. Eyes
    4. Hair: including color, length, distinctive style, facial hair
    5. Approximate age
    6. Approximate height
    7. Approximate weight
    8. Clothing
    9. Weapons
    10. Identifiable traits: including tattoos, piercings, scars, unique physical characteristics
    11. Distinctive things they said or did

Have a code name you can use if you require help, for example, "Mr. Dewey" or "Elsie Smith." One library has the code name "Bob Weber." When staff has a problem, they announce over the PA system, "Bob Weber, please come to Area 1." Staff knows what that really means is, "Security Alert! As many staff as are available, scramble to the circulation desk!" This way, patrons don't even know security has been called, and they don't realize that Area 1 is the circulation desk.

- Yell if you need to.

Be aware that some sexual acts sometimes include bodily fluids that need to be cleaned up immediately. Any body fluid including blood, saliva, vomit, and excrement needs to be treated as hazardous. The library should have appropriate cleaning supplies and hazmat gear such as the appropriate cleaners, rubber gloves, and police tape on hand at all times, and staff needs to know how to use them properly (Appendix J). If staff is not expected to do the cleanup, they need to know whom to call. The affected area should be cordoned off until it is cleaned.

Don't forget your own safety, particularly at closing time. Here, too, your local police department can advise on ways to keep your staff and yourself safe outside after hours. If you leave the library at night, walk with someone else. The shadows make perfect hiding places for sexual predators. This might even be an excellent time to practice your yelling! Is the outside lighting sufficient? Unsafe conditions are tremendous liabilities, and should never go unreported. Voice your concerns to administration. Don't forget your library's high-profile allies. They can lobby your elected officials on your behalf, citing the lack of safety, both inside and outside the library.

Although sexual deviants and predators are part of the real library world, with approved policies and procedures in place, and a lot of staff training, you can make your library safer for your staff and your customers.

In Summary

Libraries are target-rich environments for Sexual Deviates who look for quiet, concealed places to do their thing. Victims are often too mortified by the incidents to report them, or too young to know what to do about them. Working in conjunction with local police and providing staff with expert training is the best defense. Have the library evaluated for potential predator safety risks, and then correct them to take away the deviate's opportunities for seclusion and surprise. Watch for suspicious behavior and follow up on it. Post copies of the library's behavior policies in prominent places, and adopt a zero-tolerance policy for any illicit activity. Develop a code-word emergency procedure and practice it with the staff. Protect the staff's safety by adopting a closing-time policy that everyone leaves the building together after dark.

STALKERS: THE QUIET MENACES

A stalker will look for any kind of attention, positive or negative. A vast majority of them don't see themselves as stalkers.

—Jill McArthur

Libraries, by design, tend to provide suitable cover for the Stalkers who follow and harass other customers. While this isn't necessarily illegal, it does create an uncomfortable, hostile atmosphere for both staff and library users. Unless this behavior is confronted and strongly discouraged, the library risks becoming associated with this type of nuisance. A bad reputation is not only difficult to overcome, it can impact the facility's funding as well. Taxpayers demand accountability for their investment in public programs, and if customer numbers decline at a blighted facility, funding will likely follow.

Stalking behavior may be difficult to prove, because browsing in the stacks is perfectly acceptable. In fact, it's encouraged. However, Stalkers can be dangerous. If you notice people lurking for no apparent reason, approach them and ask if you can help them. If their response is vague or inappropriate, alert other staff members to keep an eye on them, too. If the lurkers begin to watch and trail specific people, notify the police, and document the incident.

Stalkers may end up being assaulters, or even murderers. Gail, a young, single woman, was a reference librarian at a metropolitan library. One day, a man showed up at the library, and began to follow her around. When she was at the reference desk, she noticed him hiding behind the stacks, staring at her. She reported this to library administration, but no actions were taken. As time went by, he got bolder. He began to follow her as she left the building. Then the unthinkable happened; Gail came home to find the man waiting for her by her front door. She asked the police for help, but she was told that the man really hadn't threatened or hurt her in any way, so there was nothing they could do. Gail moved to another state, one that was 1,300 miles away, because she could never feel safe as long as this Stalker was around. Who knew what he was capable of?

Sometimes, Stalkers will target a specific group of customers or staff members, such as teenage girls. Whether it's one person or several who are being stalked, library administration needs to take the initiative to let the Stalker know that this behavior will not be tolerated. In the case of a Stalker, copies of your documentation (see Appendix A) should be sent to the police department. (See Appendix B.) One library administrator sent this letter to a serial Stalker. Identifiable information has been deleted:

Mr. Smith:

Effective today, you are prohibited from entering any branch of the (name of library) until July 5, 2013.

On May 14, 2013, June 3, 2013, and June 4, 2013, you were observed by approximately seven Library staff and patrons to be violating the Library's Responsible Use Policy by engaging in the stalking and harassment of patrons and Library staff, and when staff attempted to confront you, you had already left the building. This behavior is unacceptable and interferes with the safe and proper functioning of the Library. Therefore, you are banned from entering any branch or grounds of the Library for one month. If you engage in this or other unacceptable behavior after you are allowed to return to the Library, additional restrictions will be placed on your access to the Library.

If you have any questions, please contact Library Administration at (phone number).

Sincerely,
(name)

This library put the Stalker on notice that he was being monitored, something a Stalker doesn't want to happen. Always treat Stalkers as dangerous. Don't use the ostrich management technique and bury your head in the proverbial sand. Pretending the Stalker will just go away doesn't work. This is an issue that needs your immediate attention. Your customers and staff deserve a safe environment.

In Summary

If a Stalker appears at your library, don't ignore him. Let him know that he is being noticed, and ask him to leave. Document encounters with Stalkers, and send copies of these reports to the police department. Don't allow a Stalker to terrorize your customers and staff.

ARSONISTS AND OTHER PYROMANIACS: FOR THE LOVE OF FIRE

> Never take a wife till thou hast a house (and a fire) to put her in.
>
> —Benjamin Franklin

The first time someone tried to torch our library, they threw burning flares into the book drop. The book drop went directly into the building, and our curtains were only a few inches away from it. It was 5:00 in the morning when the Arsonist hit, and fortunately, a waitress in the diner across the street saw the flaming curtains and called the fire department. Some damage was done, but to us, the worst of it was the smell of the smoke that seemed to cling to everything and linger forever. We closed the book chute to the inside of the library and replaced it with a proper metal outdoor container.

The second arson attempt was a few years later, when two men with criminal records started a fire in the men's restroom. That one was more contained than the first fire, but these men threatened to rape and kill the library staff person who identified them. Terrified, she moved to another state.

Arson prevention is one of those areas where you need to be diligently proactive (Appendix K). To make sure your building is as safe as possible against arson attempts arrange for the following:

- Meeting with fire department. Have staff do a walk-through of the facility with someone from your fire department. Our fire department representative pointed out potential fire hazards, and recommended that we have a floor plan with evacuation routes posted near all exits, lighted emergency exit signs, a fire extinguisher that we kept charged and checked monthly, and fire drills. Later, we installed annunciator fire alarms, which have flashing lights to alert the hearing impaired.
- Floor plan with evacuation route. First of all, make sure your floor plan is up-to-date and has accurate scale. If your library has much age to it, there's a possibility that the as-built floor plans are no longer accurate. Exits and evacuation routes should be marked. The location of the portable fire extinguisher(s), manual fire alarm box(es), fire alarm annunciators, and controls should be clearly shown. If your building has a sprinkler system, the locations of the heads and valves should also be marked.
- Lighted emergency exit signs. Check with your city and state codes to see what kind of lighted emergency exit signs you should have. Rules state the type and size of sign, illumination standards, the size and color of letters, and the material from which the sign should be fabricated, usually metal or other code-approved durable materials.
- Working fire extinguishers. The fire department will tell you what kind of fire extinguisher you need. Ours is an A-B-C type. Designate a place for the fire extinguisher that is in plain sight and easily accessible. All staff and volunteers should know where it is, and it should stay where it belongs unless it needs to be removed for an emergency. During the monthly inspection, check these things:

    1. The extinguisher is in the right place.
    2. The operating instructions are visible. The print is usually small, so copy these in a large font and post them on the wall by the extinguisher.
    3. The seal doesn't show signs of tampering.
    4. The pin lock is in place.
    5. The canister is charged. Verify this by both looking at the gauge and physically lifting the extinguisher.
    6. The canister has no physical damage. For example, are there dents that weren't noted the previous month?

7. The professional inspection date is within the last 12 months.
8. Staff initials are on the back of the inspection tag for the last month, and yours for this one.

- <u>Fire drills</u>. Be sure everyone is familiar with evacuation procedures and evacuation routes are posted by exits. Fire drills need to be random. All customers, staff, and volunteers should participate. Arrange for a meeting place, and be sure there's a record of who's there for the day so everyone can be accounted for.

You never know when you're going to need to evacuate your library. Fire isn't the only reason a library is evacuated. We've evacuated because of flooding and severe ceiling leaks where the tiles have begun to fall down. We've also evacuated because of chemical fumes that came from the outside through our intake vents. Things happen. Be prepared.

By being proactive, we might not have completely foiled potential Arsonists, but we've certainly made it harder for them to do their thing. We used what we'd learned about fire prevention when we designed our other branches. For our next library, the new main library, we built a drive-up book drop that was on a pull-out in the road adjacent to the library. Our third and final library facility is also equipped with outside book drops, so any fire would be contained. By learning from our mistakes, heeding the advice of fire prevention experts, and rectifying our problems, we made our libraries safer places for everyone.

In Summary

Be proactive with fire prevention efforts. Have a fire professional assess your facility and advise you on ways to improve fire safety and develop escape plans. Include the evacuation plan in your policy manual. Conduct unannounced fire drills to make sure all staff members are familiar with various exit routes and the designated meeting place outside the facility. Be sure exits are well marked and lit. Keep extinguishers in good working order and have them checked regularly. In the event of a fire, call the fire department immediately and activate your escape plan. Ensure that everyone is safely evacuated and notify responders if you think anyone is still inside. After the danger has passed, document as much of the incident as possible.

CRIMINALLY DANGEROUS PATRONS: WHAT YOU DON'T KNOW CAN HURT YOU

> The world is a dangerous place to live; not because of the people who are evil, but because of the people who don't do anything about it.
>
> —Albert Einstein

On November 12, 1992, librarian Kay Blanton was working alone at the Buckeye Public Library when Richard Hurles, just out of prison, came into the library and forced Ms. Blanton to lock the door. He proceeded to sexually assault her, beat her, kick her, and stab her 37 times. Her brutal murder in this peaceful town 35 miles west of Phoenix with a population of between 5,000 and 6,000 people at the time stunned the library world.

At another Arizona library, Sarah, a circulation assistant, noticed smoke coming from the men's bathroom as two men opened the door to leave. They were arrested for arson, and her positive identification of them led to their conviction. The men wrote to Sarah from prison, promising that as soon as they got out, they would "rape her and kill her." Sarah moved to a different state.

A gunman in the downtown Sacramento library went to the third floor and opened fire, killing two librarians at the reference desk. The shooter then went to the roof, where police shot him, and he fell five stories to his death.

The Salt Lake City Public Library has been the scene of violence on several occasions. To date, three people have committed suicide there. In 1994, a gunman took hostage approximately a hundred people at the library. SWAT officers shot and killed him when they stormed the room where the hostages were being held. In 2006, a homemade pipe bomb exploded in the library. Fortunately, the bomb only blew out a third-story window, and no one was injured. (See Appendix M.)

Crime can happen at any time and on any part of your library property. At 12:30 P.M. on May 22, 2012, a two-year-old boy and a seven-month-old baby were kidnapped from a library parking lot in Burien, Washington, by Michael Riley, a man high on drugs with known gang affiliations and a history of assault, domestic violence, and weapons use. He assaulted his ex-girlfriend and then fled with her car and two children. Thanks to an Amber Alert and a theft detection system in the car, four hours later, Riley was apprehended, and the children were safe. Officers said that the suspect was "high on crack" and had a .38 caliber handgun in the vehicle.

Crime near your library can affect you, too. A person down the block from our library was shooting at passersby. The police had us lock-down the library until he was caught. It's a sad truth, but you need to be prepared for the unthinkable.

Homicide remains the leading cause of deaths for women in the workplace. According to the Bureau of Labor Statistics Census of Fatal Occupational Injuries, there were 4,547 fatal workplace injuries in the United States during 2010. Of those, 506 were workplace homicides. Although total workplace homicides actually fell by 7 percent in 2010 to the lowest number ever recorded by the fatality census, workplace homicides involving women actually increased by 13 percent. Although most workplace killers are either disgruntled or former employees, or obsessed, abusive lovers or spouses, there have been instances of complete strangers walking into a library and killing someone. At any point, your library can be an environment ripe for violence.

Drug abuse, alcohol abuse, Post-Traumatic Stress Disorder (PTSD), and domestic disputes can all produce violent behavior. Be alert to employee concerns about potentially Dangerous People and situations. As a manager, failure to act on these warnings makes you directly liable should your library become the scene of preventable violence. Patron safety is paramount. Ensure that your facility has adequate security, trust your gut, and listen to your employees and patrons. Day and night, they are your eyes and ears in the stacks, on the premises and even in the parking lot. Never allow their concerns to go uninvestigated. You just might save a life, maybe even your own.

In many ways, libraries are ideal places to commit crimes. The very features that make them desirable also make them dangerous. Often comfortable, unsupervised nooks and crannies, multiple rooms with lockable doors, and rows of shelving interfere with the librarian's line of sight. The most vulnerable customers, women and children are generally considered easy targets by criminals, and comprise the largest percentage of regular library customers. A 2011 American Library Association (ALA) report on library usage reveals 65 percent of those polled said they had visited their library in the past year. Women are significantly more likely to visit the library than men (72 percent vs. 58 percent), and most of them are either working women, working mothers, or women aged 18–54 (ALA Library Fact Sheet 6). Even when a crime occurs, people have become so conditioned to the notion that libraries are quiet places it's not unusual for victims to remain silent when bad things happen.

Extremely Dangerous People can be very unpredictable, act with little or no warning, and leave no time to prepare. For this reason, library directors, managers, and supervisors need to be proactive to prevent dangerous situations using the following methods:

- Listen to staff concerns about patron or staff behavior. Take action, if necessary. Document carefully. Include date, time, place, who was there, and how the problem was addressed.
- Take all situations seriously. A small argument can escalate very quickly, and you never know which customers might be carrying weapons.
- Don't assume that because your library is in a "nice" part of town your staff or customers won't be the victims of violence.
- Avoid scheduling yourself or your staff to work alone in the building.
- Work with the police to improve your security. Ask them to perform a Crime Prevention through Environmental Design (CPTED) analysis of your facility. This process identifies risk factors, both physical and in practice.
- Have you made your working environment as safe as possible? Identify secluded spaces in the building and consider ways to make them more open and accessible.
- Is the lighting adequate? Have the facilities manager check your light levels to ensure they're adequate. This is as much a safety concern as it is a security risk.
- Do you need surveillance equipment? Areas that can't be made more accessible could benefit from surveillance equipment. Also consider this equipment for areas that are prone to theft or vandalism.
- Do you have a clean line of sight? Arrange stacks and displays for maximum line of sight from any occupied work area.
- Do you practice good record-keeping? Documenting all complaints and incidents provides a history for repeat offenders who could be subject to legal action if dangerous behaviors persist.
- Do you have, and use, incident report forms? (See Appendix A.) Maintain an electronic template for staff use, or access the local police department website for additional resources.
- Are you adhering to police recommendations from your library's CPTED? Ignoring recommendations can result in liability if a preventable incident occurs.
- Is your security training ongoing? Like anything else, training that isn't practiced or reinforced is soon forgotten. Periodic refreshers on safety precautions and procedures will keep staff informed and prepared.
- Do you have police-approved disaster plans in place, and is your staff familiar with them?
- Do you have a staff safety committee that regularly reviews safety procedures and potential dangers?

It is your job as supervisor or manager to see that procedures are in place so staff can protect themselves and others in the library. Train staff and volunteers on what to do during dangerous situations. All staff, all levels, no exceptions. Training should include role-playing, and, as odd as it seems, have your staff practice shouting. This could be something as simple as "IT'S OKAY TO YELL IN THE LIBRARY!" Remember, they've been conditioned, too.

Ask your police or sheriff's department to demonstrate the proper way to describe both the Dangerous Patron and the situation during a 911 call (Appendix B).

If your situation calls for it, and your budget can afford it, think about hiring security guards. They, too, should be trained on your adopted safety procedures. In the large, regional libraries in Maricopa County, Arizona, the guards are even armed, and have been since the late 1990s. Be selective of the security services you hire. Bear in mind that incompetent security guards, a possibility with low-bid situations, may create more problems than they solve.

Adopt a policy that staff members who work the late shift should leave the library as a group when the library closes. Crimes against individuals are more likely to occur than crimes against a group of people.

If a traumatic event occurs at your library, be sure to offer assistance to the victim(s) and, if necessary, grief counseling. It's likely your police or fire department employs professional counselors who can help your staff and patrons deal with the emotional fallout of witnessing a violent act.

The authors have provided you with a variety of examples of situations where they have and where you and your staff may encounter problem patrons. They have also provided policy statements for some of those situations. During our writing of this book, several librarians have offered policy statements to cover situations with problem patrons. The ones you will find in Appendix N may be helpful to you as you review and rewrite your policies.

In Summary

Don't delude yourself into thinking that nothing violent will ever happen in your library. Just ask any victim what they used to think. It's not so much a matter of "if" but "when." Be prepared.

PART VIII

Appendices

APPENDIX A

Incident Report Form: Using an Incident Report

If it isn't documented, it didn't happen!

—unknown

We strongly recommend that a library use an Incident Report Form for reporting any situation involving unacceptable behavior by the public, injury or possible injury to staff or the public, and any situation that might create a liability for the library or the city of which the library forms a part.

The forms should be readily available to all staff—for example, in hard copy at each work location, or in a shared folder on the library's Intranet site. Due to greater flexibility and the ease of communication, the electronic format is preferred, but if your library doesn't have an Intranet, a hard copy version works just fine. Strongly encourage all staff to fill out and submit an Incident Report for any incident, or for any occurrence that might possibly become an incident.

At our library, the reports are kept in a shared file, where any staff member can find previous incident reports. New reports are distributed to an email group named "IncidentReports." This group includes:

- Library supervisors. Library supervisors need to be aware of, and ready to respond to, any incidents involving the staff they oversee. A given incident might trigger reassignment of staff members or additional security measures.
- Library administrators. Administrators need to be informed of what's happening in the public area of the library so they can recommend and fund future preventative measures.
- Library safety committee. The library has a safety committee that meets regularly to review safety concerns of the library system and make recommendations to the library administration. Receiving these incident reports give them guidance for their recommendations.
- All staff. Every staff member at every branch needs to be informed of incidents. People who cause problems at one branch often cause problems at other branches too. If patrons are barred from one branch, they are considered barred from all branches; yet, they may go to another branch to try to gain access. All staff need to be aware of, and watch for, these people.

113

- Risk Management. The City has an office of Risk Management. It is important that personnel trained in managing liability be aware of occurrences that could create a possible liability for the City or the library.
- Police Department. The library has a working relationship with the City police department. A few specific officers from the police department are assigned as liaisons to the library. Each of these liaisons receives a copy of each incident report so that they are aware of potential risks to persons or property and can take preventative measures against future incidents.

Staff members are expected to submit a report as soon as possible after an incident occurs so that events are fresh in their memory and so that word gets out to others as soon as possible. Additionally, they are encouraged to go back and amend the report as needed. If more than one staff member is involved, participation by each staff member is encouraged. Each staffer may submit an individual report or they may work together to submit a group report. All reports are kept in the shared folder on the library Intranet so any of those mentioned above can access the folder to refer back to a prior incident at any time.

If an incident involves a registered library patron who can be identified, a brief comment is made in the patron's record in the online circulation system. These comments "pop up" and display at the time the patron's file is accessed so that staff know that there has been an incident involving this person. The note also includes the phrase "See IR [Incident Report] #XXXX" so that staff are quickly able to get more detail.

One section of the incident report form appears in red in the online version due to its importance: "Action taken and/or recommendation for action" because the staff member reporting the incident is probably the person closest to and with the greatest knowledge of the situation, his or her recommendation is highly important. This recommendation is then seen by all the decision makers involved in the process: library supervisors and administrators, the safety committee, the office of Risk Management, and the police department, thus assuring a great chance of prevention of future occurrences.

STOCKTON-SAN JOAQUIN COUNTY PUBLIC LIBRARY

INCIDENT REPORT

OUTLET/SECTION: _____   Date of incident: _____   Time: _____

Narrative and description of incident. Include the following information to support the statement:

➢ Name of person(s) involved, with addresses and telephone numbers
➢ Type of incident (e.g., complaints, building problems, improper behavior—include a complete description of the person, etc.)
➢ Action taken (e.g., police called; parents notified; ambulance requested; etc.)
➢ Recommendations for further action

THIS REPORT DOES NOT NEED TO BE TYPED. WRITE LEGIBLY.
USE REVERSE SIDE FOR FURTHER EXPLANATION.

Describe the incident:

Action taken and/or recommendation for action:

Reporting Staff Member _____   **Date of Report** _____

Supervisor (if available) _____

Supervising Librarian _____

Send Incident Report to the Supervising Librarian within one (1) day of occurrence. Report emergencies/major incidents immediately, either in person or by telephone before completing this form. Forward as indicated below.

Stockton: Incidents involving public health and safety are referred to the Stockton Police Dept. _____
(Forwarding to Incident Reports also forwards to Stockton Police Department)   Initials/date

County: Refer public health and safety to local law enforcement.   _____
          Initials/date

APPENDIX B

Involving the Authorities: Things to Consider

If you witness a crime or suspect criminal activity is in progress, use caution and good judgment in the actions you choose, to avoid endangering yourself and your customers. Calling the police should be your first resort, not your last. Take personal responsibility for making the call. Don't presume someone else will have the presence of mind to do it. Observe as many details as you can and be prepared to provide them to the dispatcher.

Remember, the dispatcher is trained to perform this service and follows a defined dispatch protocol. The person you speak to probably takes hundreds of emergency calls a week. Let them lead you through the reporting process, even if it seems repetitious and futile. While they're taking your statement, they're also summoning help. Be calm, be patient, be professional.

What is your emergency? This is the first question the dispatcher will ask. Explain what you saw or what was observed by another witness. If the incident is still in progress, be sure the dispatcher knows this too. If you're uncertain about some of the details, say so. Describe the event succinctly and factually, and don't obscure important details with embellishment or exaggeration. It serves no purpose.

What is your location? Your address will be your first reply, followed by where on the premises the incident occurred.

What time did the incident occur? In all the excitement a detail like this is easily missed. But if the call is placed immediately after the incident, or while it's in progress, the approximate time will be automatically recorded in the dispatch system.

Is anyone hurt? If the incident involves injured people paramedic services will be needed. In a typical 911 system, the police dispatch center is also the primary contact for emergency medical services. The police dispatcher will walk you through this process. At some point you will be asked to explain the type and extent of injuries so paramedics will know what to expect on arrival and if an ambulance is needed. You will also be asked how many people are injured, so the dispatcher will know the number and types of resources to send. You may also be instructed how to assist the injured until the paramedics arrive.

How many people were involved? Was the incident the act of a single person, or were there others involved? Here is where your powers of observation will be tested. Describe the suspect(s).

- Gender
- Race
- Eyes
- Hair: including color, length, distinctive style, facial hair
- Approximate age
- Approximate height
- Approximate weight
- Clothing
- Weapons
- Identifiable traits: including tattoos, piercings, scars, unique physical characteristics
- Distinctive things they said or did

Did they leave the premises? If the person left before police arrived, you'll need to note the details of their departure as well.

- Which way did they go?
- Did they drive?
- What kind of vehicle? Year, make, model, color.
- Did anyone see the license plate?
- Were there any identifiable marks on the car?

APPENDIX C

COMPUTER USAGE BY PATRONS BUCKEYE, ARIZONA PUBLIC LIBRARY "ELECTRONIC RESOURCES POLICY"

A. Introduction

The goal of the Buckeye Public Library is to provide residents access to knowledge through technological resources which assist them in meeting their informational, recreational, educational and cultural needs. Our Library staff is dedicated to providing services to users in a professional, timely and courteous manner.

A Buckeye Public Library card is required to use the Library's public access computers. Out of town visitors may use computers by presenting a valid form of identification, as listed in the Circulation Policy section.

The Library reserves the right to change or modify, without notice, the nature of access to specific electronic resources to better serve the citizens of Buckeye.

B. Limitation of Liability

1. Internet Access

The Buckeye Public Library provides access to the Internet in order to enable the Library and its users to obtain a vast array of information not available in the Library collection. The Internet provides a gateway to information from many countries and cultures of the world. While the Internet generally provides access to information that is valuable and enlightening, the user may find information that is controversial, offensive, disturbing, erroneous, or illegal. In accordance with the Arizona state statute (A.R.S §34–502), the Buckeye Public Library uses a filtering device on public computers in order to limit a minor's ability to gain access to material deemed harmful to minors under A.R.S. §13–3501 et seq. Filtering software may not block all material that some users may find offensive. The Library does not monitor, and does not have complete control over information accessed through the Internet and cannot be held responsible for content, presentation, or its use.

The Library affirms the right and responsibility of parents and guardians to determine and monitor their children's use of library materials and resources, including the Internet. Restriction of a child's access to the Internet is the responsibility of parents and guardians. Parents are encouraged to read My Rules of Online Safety and the Child Safety on the Information Highway published by the National Center for Missing and Exploited Children.

C. Security and Privacy

Data downloaded from external computers and networks, including the Internet, may contain computer viruses that could be potentially harmful to the computer systems of Library users. The Buckeye Public Library is not responsible for damage to any user's storage media or computer, or any loss of data, damage, or liability that may occur from a library user's utilization of the Library's electronic information resources. The Library recommends that users maintain checking and scanning software to identify and eliminate viruses in any data, files, or programs they obtain from external computers and networks.

Use of the Library's wireless network is entirely at the risk of the user and the Buckeye Public Library disclaims all liability for any damage that may occur to one's computer and/or loss of confidential information or other damages resulting from that loss. As with most public 'hot spots,' the library's connection is not secure. Users accessing the wireless network should have personal firewall and updated virus protection software installed on their computers to protect their privacy and to provide for their own security. Any information being sent or received could potentially be intercepted by another wireless user. Users should avoid entering credit card numbers, passwords or any other confidential information unless they are certain that the Website they are using provides its own security mechanism such as a Secure Sockets Layer 'SSL' encoding. An SSL protected web page is usually indicated by a small lock icon display at the lower edge of the browser window.

D. Use of Copyrighted Materials

The Buckeye Public Library provides access to copyrighted materials, including copyrighted electronic materials. Responsibility for the consequence of copyright infringement shall lie with the Library user. Under certain conditions specified in the law (Title 17, United States Code), libraries and archives are authorized to furnish a photocopy or other reproduction. One of these specified conditions is that the photocopy or reproduction is not to be "used for any purpose other than private study, scholarship, or research" (17 U.S.C.A. § 108). If a user makes a request for, or later uses, a photocopy or reproduction for purposes in excess of "fair use," that user may be liable for copyright infringement. The Library reserves the right to refuse to accept a copying order, if, in its judgment, fulfillment of the order would involve violation of copyright law.

The Library expressly disclaims liability or responsibility resulting from copyright infringement by users.

B. Responsibilities

1. User Responsibilities

All electronic resources may only be used for legal purposes; per federal order (F.C.C. 03–188), filtering software is applied to all computers. Examples of possible illegal use include, but are not limited to, the following:

- Attempting to alter or damage computer equipment, software configurations, or files belonging to the Library, other users or external networks
- Attempting unauthorized entry to the Library's network or external networks
- Intentional propagation of computer viruses
- Violation of Federal copyright or telecommunications laws (A.R.S. 13–3707)
- Violation of software license agreements
- Transmission of speech not protected by the first amendment
- Display of materials considered obscene as defined by the Neighborhood Children's Internet Protection Act, Pub. L. 106–554, and as defined by A.R.S. section 13–3501 through 13–3512; especially statues 13–3501, 13–3506 and 13–3507

- Gambling on the Internet; Internet gambling is not amusement, social or regulated gambling as defined by A.R.S. 13–3304.
- Violation of any Federal, Arizona State or Town of Buckeye laws.

2. Ethical Standards

Electronic resources must also be used in accordance with the ethical standards of the Library. Examples of unethical use (which may also have legal consequences) include, but are not limited to, the following:

- Violation of computer system security
- Unauthorized use of computer accounts or access codes assigned to others
- Using computer communications in ways that tie-up, interfere with, or impede other's computer usage
- Violation of external network regulations and policies
- Violation of another user's privacy

3. Guidelines for Use

- When using electronic resources at the Library:
  - Library users shall have access to the Library's public access computers on a first-come, first-served basis.
  - Library users must present a valid Buckeye Public Library card or valid identification to make a computer reservation.
  - Workstations are allocated for 30 minute time slots. Time extensions will be granted based on availability and scheduling. Patrons must relinquish usage of a workstation when asked by a Library staff member. Failure to do so will result in the loss of computer-use privileges, potential loss of Library privilege and potential legal consequences.
  - Computers located in the Teen/Children are for the exclusive use of children under the age of eighteen.
  - Library computers shall not be used to participate in gambling activities.
  - The Library does not provide personal email accounts, however, there are some sites on the World Wide Web that provide email accounts free of charge.
  - Library users shall not, in accordance with Arizona law (A.R.S. §13-3507), use the Library's electronic information systems for the public display of explicit sexual materials.
  - Library users shall not, in accordance with Arizona law and Library policy, use the Library's electronic information systems for the public display of material harmful to minors.
  - A variety of print services are available to Library users. Users may select from the following list of services and fees: black and white prints or copies at ten (10) cents per page; color prints at seventy-five (75) cents per page and faxes at $1.00 per page. Fees are subject to change. Printers are not available via our wireless network.

C. Sanctions

Library users who violate the Buckeye Public Library's Electronic Resource policy, will be removed from the Library, and may have their library privileges revoked. Violations of the policies described above regarding the legal and ethical use of the Library's electronic information resources will be dealt with in a serious and appropriate manner. Illegal acts involving the Library's electronic resources may be subject to prosecution by local, state, or federal authorities.

D. Responsibilities of the Library

1. Staff Assistance

Library staff will be pleased to assist users in accessing its electronic information resources as service demands permit. Each user is, however, ultimately responsible for his or her own search. Staff cannot provide in-depth individual training in the use of the Internet or personal computers. Computer Basics classes are offered throughout the year, free of charge. Please check with the front desk for a schedule and to sign up.

Patrons using their personal laptop computers to access the Internet via the Library's wireless network are responsible for setting up their own equipment. Basic instructions are available for accessing the Internet via the wireless network. Library staff cannot assist with a laptop card or configuration issues.

2. Freedom of Speech

The Buckeye Public Library believes strongly in the free flow of information and resources and makes every effort to comply with the First Amendment of the United States Constitution and Article II, Section 6 of the Arizona Constitution. Accordingly, any visitor to the Library who uses the electronic information resources and reasonably believes that the Library's filtering software had unnecessarily blocked a Website can seek to have it reviewed expeditiously by Library staff. If the Library staff determines the Website to be in violation of the policy, the visitor can request further expeditious review by staff at the Town Attorney's office. If the staff at the Town Attorney's office determines the Website to be in violation of the policy, the visitor can request further expeditious judicial review of said Website. If the Library staff or Town Attorney's office determine that the Website is not in violation of the policy, Library staff will promptly submit a request to the Information Technology department to modify the filter so that it will permit access to the site in question. If a visitor to the Library using the Library's electronic resources finds a Website that he or she feels is in violation of the policy and that has not been blocked by the filter, the visitor can seek to have it reviewed expeditiously by Library staff. If the Library staff or Town Attorney's office determine that the reported Website is in violation of the policy, Library staff will promptly submit a request to the Information Technology department to modify the filter so that it will not permit access to the site in question. The aforementioned procedural safeguards are not a license to purposely offend Library staff, and any attempt to do so may result in the loss of library privileges.

4. Notice

The Buckeye Public Library shall provide notice of the provisions of this policy and make available both electronic and paper copies of this policy.

COMPUTER USAGE BY PATRONS: CHILLICOTHE PUBLIC LIBRARY—ILLINOIS "COMPUTER USAGE—COMPUTER USE BY PATRONS"

1) Computers have been purchased using various grant funds. The library staff maintains the equipment and software for public use. Downloading of any software is prohibited.
2) Public use of the equipment must be shared with the library staff. Patrons have to sign a log sheet at the circulation desk before using any equipment. Patron use is limited to 30 minutes per day if other patrons are waiting to use the computer.

3) If necessary, the sign up log sheet will be used to determine the order of usage by patrons.

4) The library card catalog has been inputted to the Public Access Catalog. ASK THE LIBRARY STAFF FOR ASSISTANCE IN ACCESSING THE PUBLIC ACCESS CATALOG.

5) Public use of the equipment for writing letters, resumes, doing homework, or other applications is possible under the following conditions:

    a) Patrons must provide their own disks if they want to store any input. They will not be permitted to place information on the hard disk drive

    b) Patrons must have what is to be inputted completely ready for entry to minimize actual time on the computer

    c) Patrons are to proof their work on the screen. One printed copy of their work will be allowed free of charge. Additional copies will be assessed a charge per page

6) Printouts from databases and CD-ROMs after the first four (4) pages will be assessed a $.25 per sheet charge. Patrons are asked to have additional copies made on the photocopy machine.

7) Patrons may not load personal computer programs on to the Library equipment. READ ONLY disks will be permitted if they are properly formatted and compatible with Library computers. They must be approved by the library staff at the time the patron signs the log sheet before using the equipment.

Children's Rules

1) Sign the log sheet at the librarian's desk;

2) If computers or programs are altered or damaged, the patron will be billed for the repairs;

3) The user has a 30 minute per session use limit if other patrons are waiting to use the computer.

Internet Access

Library Internet Policy and Agreement

Welcome! We are pleased to be able to offer Internet access in our Library! Please read the following policy carefully as it discusses the Library's rules and regulations regarding Internet use in the Library and in compliance with federal law. Your cooperation is appreciated.

Users Guide to the Internet as a Resource

Remember the Internet is a collection of information not produced nor endorsed by the Library. The Internet has become an invaluable tool for research, communication, and entertainment. However, please keep the following in mind.

1. Information obtained via the Internet may or may not be reliable and may or may not be obtained from a reliable source.

    1. Information obtained via the Internet may or may not be accurate.

    2. Information obtained via the Internet may or may not be current.

    3. Information obtained via the Internet may be considered controversial or offensive by some Library patrons.

This Library encourages all Library patrons to be informed users and carefully evaluate any information obtained via the Internet. Library staff members may help you evaluate certain types of Internet sources, but are not trained to provide definitive analysis of specific sources or sites.

This Library is not responsible for damages, indirect or direct, arising from a Library patrons' reliance, citation, or other utilization of Internet information resources.

Internet Filtration

All Library computers are equipped with Internet filtration devices which are designed and intended to block sites deemed to be inappropriate for general audiences. Adults (over the age of 16) may request that a certain site be unblocked, for bona fide research or other lawful purposes. Granting such a request is ALWAYS up to the discretion of the Library staff and may be denied for any reason in order to comply with Library policy or otherwise. Minors under the age of 17 years old are not allowed to access a computer with unfiltered Internet access at any time. Minors under the age of 17 years old may NOT accompany an adult who is accessing a computer with unfiltered Internet access at any time.

All Internet filtration devices installed on Library computers have been purchased from a commercial vendor. The Library does not maintain that the installed filters effectively filter all or any inappropriate materials from access within the Library. The Library is not responsible for damages, indirect or direct, arising from access, whether voluntarily or involuntarily requested, to inappropriate or offensive Internet sites within the Library, regardless of the age of the user or whether arising from the deficiency of the filter or its installation.

Access and Use of the Library's Internet Connections and Networks by Adults

The Library recognizes that electronic information on the Internet may contain material that is inappropriate or offensive to children as well as patrons of all ages. The Library requires that all Library patrons using the Library's Internet connection do so within the guidelines of appropriate and acceptable use. The following are unacceptable:

1. Any use of electronic information which results in the harassment of others;
2. Use of electronic information networks in any way which violates a Federal or State law;
3. Unauthorized duplication of protected software or licensing agreements, including but not exclusively, any "hacking;"
4. Destruction or damage to or unauthorized alteration of the Library's computer equipment;
5. Behaving in a manner that is disruptive to others;
6. Accessing child pornography;
7. Accessing material depicting offensive sexual conduct which lacks a high level of artistic, political, or scientific value; and
8. Any unauthorized disclosure, use and dissemination of personal identification information regarding minors. The Library reserves the right to classify any action, access, or operation on the Internet inappropriate and ban its use by patrons.

Access and Use of the Library's Internet Connections and Networks by Minors Under the Age of 17

All access and use restrictions applicable to adults are also applicable to minors. In addition, the following are specifically unacceptable for minors:

1. Accessing any inappropriate matter on the Internet; and
2. Accessing any picture, image, visual depiction, description, or representation exhibiting qualities of nudity or sexual acts or contact. Exceptions are rare and are only appropriate when images possess overwhelming artistic, political, or scientific value.
3. Accessing any computer within the Library at any time which does not have an active Internet filtration device in place.

The Library reserves the right to classify any action, access, or operation on the Internet inappropriate and ban its use by minor patrons.

Parents are expected to monitor and supervise their children's use of the Internet in the Library. Parents are encouraged to discuss with their children issues of appropriate use and Internet safety. Please be advised that the Library does NOT filter all websites deemed to be inappropriate for very young children. Advanced filtration may be available for young children desiring Internet access.

Privacy on the Internet

The Library will make every effort to allow Library patrons to privately use the Internet in the Library. However, the Library is mandated by federal law to provide for monitoring a minor's use of Internet access, and therefore the Library reserves the right to supervise minor's, under the age of 17, as well as all patrons' use of the Internet to reasonably ensure compliance with Library Internet policies by all patrons. The Library reserves the right to request an explanation or otherwise inquire as to when a patron is found to be accessing material a Library staff member reasonably believes to be beyond compliance with Library Internet policy.

Email, Instant Messaging and Internet Chat

It is the policy of the Library to permit its users to engage in forms of direct electronic communication known as electronic mail ("Email"), instant messaging and Internet chat. However, such use by minors under the age of 17 may be monitored from time to time and in the event Library staff believe a minor's safety or security is at risk, such privileges will be suspended or revoked.

Violation of Policy

The violation of any terms of the Library's policy may result in suspension or revocation of Library Internet access privileges or even the suspension or revocation of general Library use privileges. Please act responsibly!

Internet Filtration Warning

All Library computers are equipped with Internet filtration devices which are designed and intended to block sites deemed to be inappropriate for general audiences. These devices have been purchased from a commercial vendor. The Library does not maintain that the installed filters effectively filter all or any inappropriate materials from access within the Library. The Library is not responsible for damages, indirect or direct, arising from access, whether voluntarily or involuntarily requested, to inappropriate or offensive Internet sites, regardless of the age of the user or whether arising from the deficiency of the filter or its installation.

Library Staff CANNOT assist patrons in any capacity with . . .

- Filling out Job Applications or Resumes
- Filling out TAX forms or offering TAX advice
- Online Billing or Customer Account issues for any company billing to any personal, business or private Accounts (cell phones, utilities, credit cards, cable, etc.)
- Setting up or assisting with accounts for any Social Networking or Dating website
- Filling out forms to set up a new e-mail account
- Fixing problems with e-mail accounts
- Accessing, fixing, altering, inputting information or giving ADVICE for ANY patron's PERSONAL, PRIVATE OR PASSWORD protected information or accounts.
  (restrictions may not be limited to the above mentioned list and may be added at the Tech's discretion)

Library Staff CAN assist patrons with . . .

- any questions about the use of the public computers (themselves)
- questions about CPLD's Public Computer Policy
- help with computer programs or publicly accessible websites or programs that are NOT password protected
- help with accessing patron's personal media (thumb drives, disks, etc.)

- questions about and help with printing documents to the library printer located at the Circulation Desk
- accessing the Library's wireless network

Internet Usage Agreement

Name (Please Print)

_____ Last First

Registration and User Agreement

1. I have read the policies concerning the use of the Internet in the Library;
2. I understand that copyright laws restrict the duplication of copyrighted materials and will follow all copyright laws;
3. I understand that if I fail to abide by the Library's Internet policies I can lose my eligibility for use of this service or even use of the Library;
4. I understand and acknowledge that the Internet contains material of a controversial nature [Option: including pornography, obscenity, excessive violence, inflammatory or dangerous material], and that the Library has no control over the Internet and assumes no responsibility for the content, quality, accuracy, appropriateness of any Internet resources; and
5. I understand that the filters installed on the Library computers may or may not be effective in blocking voluntary or involuntary access to inappropriate or offensive material and, by this agreement, release and discharge the Library from any direct or indirect liability resulting from such access.

_____ Date: _____ Signature

For Patrons Under the Age of 17:

As the parent or guardian of _____

I give permission for my child to use the Internet connection at the Library, with the understanding that I am responsible for monitoring my child's appropriate use of this service and that I am responsible for any damages that may occur and that I have read, understand, and agree to the above statements, specifically including any deficiencies in the performance or installation of blocking filters.

Parent or Guardian Signature: _____ Date: _____

APPENDIX D

A. The following conduct, behaviors, or resulting effects are not permitted within the library.

1. Disorderly behavior of any kind, including yelling, excessive noise, running in the building, or otherwise causing a disruption to the peace and order of the library. Note: This policy does not prohibit quiet conversation between patrons and/or staff members or conversations required to carry on library programs or business. It is designed to preserve a reasonably quiet atmosphere where library patrons may study and otherwise use library materials without disturbance.

2. Use of a cellular phone, audible pager, audio equipment, audio-visual equipment, or similar equipment so that it disturbs others. For the courtesy of other library users, cell phones must be turned off or set to vibrate upon entering the building. Cell phone conversations should be held outside the building.

3. Abandonment of individuals, both adults and children, who are unable to take care of themselves. A responsible adult must attend children under the age of eight (8) years. The responsible adult must be close enough to both see and hear the child.

4. Vandalizing or defacing library materials or property including books, audio-visual materials, furniture, walls, computer equipment or facilities. State Statuary reference A.R.S. 13–1602.

5. Removing library materials, equipment or property from the building without proper checkout or authorization.

6. Indecent exposure, voyeurism, exhibitionism, or other lewd or lascivious acts. State Statuary reference A.R.S. 13–1402, 13–1404 AND 13–1424.

7. Putting feet or legs on library furniture; rearranging or disarranging library furnishings and equipment.

8. Bringing firearms or other deadly weapons into the building. State Statuary reference A.R.S. 13–3102.

9. Harassment of library users or staff, either verbally or through actions. This may include abuse, use of profanity or other abusive language whether verbal or written toward other library users or toward library employees, intimidation, staring at or following another

person in the library with the effect of annoying a person of reasonable sensibilities, sexual harassment or harassment on account of religion, ethnic background, gender, or sexual orientation.

10. Violating the provisions of the Electronic Resources Policy.
11. Not wearing shoes or a shirt.
12. Bringing a bicycle into the building. Bicycles must be secured in the rack provided.
13. Using skateboards, in-line skates, roller skates (incl. Heelies), scooters, or other sports equipment within the library building.
14. Bringing animals into the building, except those used to assist an individual with a disability.
15. Sleeping in the library; using restrooms for washing clothes or bathing.
16. Bringing bedrolls, suitcases, blankets, shopping carts, and similar articles into the library.
17. Smoking or other uses of tobacco or tobacco products in the library.
18. Possessing or consuming alcohol or illegal drugs, or being under the influence of alcohol or illegal drugs. State Statuary reference A.R.S. 13–3401 et seq.
19. Gambling. State Statuary reference A.R.S. 13–3301 et seq.
20. Blocking library entrances or exits.
21. Selling products or services, soliciting for personal gain; or approaching library users for the purpose of obtaining signatures for petitions within the building.
22. Leaving personal property in the library unattended. The library is not responsible for lost, damaged, or stolen property.
23. Violation of any ordinances, laws, or regulations of the Town of Buckeye, the State of Arizona, or any of its political subdivisions, or of the United States. Penalties: Violations of the above policy guidelines can result in a verbal warning, ejection from the Library by a member of the Library staff; or loss of library privileges, including borrowing privileges, and access to the library building. Failure to comply with the policy after being notified of a violation by a library staff member may result in the Buckeye Police Department being summoned and violators being prosecuted in accordance with applicable ordinances or laws.

BEHAVIOR POLICIES/RULES OF CONDUCT: SCOTTSDALE PUBLIC LIBRARY—ARIZONA "RULES OF CONDUCT"

Policy Manual
Public Library System Rules of Conduct

Policy Statement:

It is the policy of the Scottsdale Public Library System to maintain a safe environment in all library facilities. Our goal is to provide a positive experience where all library users are ensured open access to library services and programs.

Regulations:

1. Be considerate and respectful of all library users and staff, and behave in a manner that does not disturb other persons. Unacceptable conduct includes, but is not limited to:

   A. Loud, disruptive and other inappropriate behavior that would be annoying to a reasonable person using library services
   B. Damaging or stealing library property
   C. Sleeping

      D. Use of any tobacco product

      E. Possession of firearms, weapons or illegal substance

2. Food and non-alcoholic beverages with lids are permitted.
3. Treat library property (materials, furnishings and equipment, etc.) with respect.
4. Dress appropriately; shirt and shoes required. Persons whose bodily hygiene is offensive so as to constitute a nuisance to other persons shall be required to leave the building.
5. Supervise your children and assist them in observing appropriate conduct.
6. Silence your cell phone or other electronic device and do not use in a manner that disturbs others.
7. Leave bicycles and gasoline-powered vehicles outside.
8. Carry or keep under a table or out of the aisles all skateboards, roller blades and other personal items.
9. Personal items are not to be left unattended. Carry or keep items with you at all times. The Library is not responsible for items left unattended.
10. Comply with staff requests in regard to library policies.
11. Assistance dogs are the only animals permitted in the library.
12. Deadly weapons are not permitted in any library facility unless specifically authorized by law.

Weapons may be secured in weapon lockers where provided.

Noncompliance with the Rules of Conduct may result in expulsion from the Library and/or suspension of library privileges.

Rev. Date: 09-17-08 Pol. No.: CUS-1

Adopted by the Library Board 01-17-01

(CUS-1) Page 1 of 1

BEHAVIOR POLICIES/RULES OF CONDUCT: CARY MEMORIAL LIBRARY—LEXINGTON, MASSACHUSETTS "RULES OF BEHAVIOR"

General Principles and Purpose

The Cary Memorial Library is supported by the taxes and the charitable contributions of the people of Lexington, MA. Our users can expect the library to be a clean, comfortable, and welcoming place for reading, researching, studying, and attending library or community sponsored programs and meetings. To this end, the Trustees of the Cary Memorial Library have established these Rules of Behavior to ensure the rights and safety of library users and staff, and to preserve and protect the library's materials, equipment, facilities, and grounds. These rules, along with other library policies, will be applied in a fair and reasonable manner.

Respect for other library users and library staff members shall be maintained at all times. Disruptive or inappropriate behavior that infringes on others' use or right to use the library shall not be permitted. The library staff reserves the right to determine if other actions not listed below constitute "disruptive or inappropriate behavior".

Individuals who will not respect these expectations may be asked to leave the library, have library privileges suspended, or be subject to legal action.

Examples of disruptive or inappropriate behavior include (but are not limited to):

    a. Smoking, using alcohol, or any other controlled substance while on library property.

b. Loud talking, loud audio equipment, use of profanity, running, throwing things, hitting, pushing or shoving.

c. Stealing, damaging, altering, or inappropriate use of the library facilities, collection, or technology.

d. Distributing written leaflets, collecting signatures for petitions, or soliciting patrons within the library facility, in the parking lot, or on walkways immediately adjacent to the library entrances. (Such activities may be conducted a reasonable distance from the library entrances in order not to impede entrance into and egress from the library.)

e. Using personal electronic equipment, such as CD players, Ipods, MP3 players, laptop computers, and cell phones in a manner that disturbs other library users. Devices that play music may be used with headphones so long as the volume does not disturb others. Cell phones may be used so long as their use does not disturb others. Those holding loud or extended conversations will be asked to use their cell phones in the lobbies or outside.

f. Using the public rest rooms as a laundry or for bathing.

g. Using the Meeting Room kitchen for personal use.

h. Excessive public displays of affection.

i. Indecent exposure/public indecency.

j. Interfering with others' use of the library, its services and materials.

k. Interfering with library staff members' ability to perform their responsibilities.

To Ensure That The Library Is A Clean, Welcoming Environment For All:

- Beverages in covered containers are permitted in most areas of the library. They are not, however, allowed in the Genealogy Room or at the public computers.

- Food is limited to the South Lobby and to approved events in the Meeting Room and Learning Center.

- Appropriate attire, including shirts and shoes, should be worn by patrons of all ages. Examples of inappropriate footwear include roller skates, roller blades, cleats and golf shoes.

- Walkways throughout the building and access to library materials should not be obstructed. Sports equipment, musical instruments and other bulky objects brought into the library should not obstruct access to library materials nor block walkways throughout the building.

- Power cords should not cross pathways or be used in ways that create a trip hazard.

- Animals, except for guide or assistance animals, are not permitted.

- Library staff members are not responsible for patrons' personal belongings left unattended.

- The telephones at all service desks are business phones. They may only be used by patrons, with staff permission, in cases of emergency or to call home for rides if the patron does not have money for the public telephone.

- The library reserves the right to inspect all bags, purses, briefcases, backpacks, etc., for concealed library material.

- The material and equipment in the library are here for patron and staff use. Any purposeful damage done to the material, equipment, furniture, building or property of the library is against the law and will be reported to the police.

- The use of study rooms and meeting rooms is limited to those who have signed up.

- Bicycles should be placed in the bike rack and locked. Bikes, scooters, or Segways may not be left inside the library or on the handicap ramp leading into the library.

- Patrons should not bring personal property into the library that the library staff considers to be hazardous. The library staff may refuse to permit a patron to have access to the library in such circumstances.

- Photography within the library is only allowed by permission of the Director, Assistant Director, or the staff member in charge, with the exception of patrons photographing their own family members. Photography within the library must not disrupt other patrons or staff.

Children In The Library

The library staff and Trustees have made Cary Library a warm and inviting place for children to develop a love of books, reading, and libraries. The Children's Room contains a wide range of materials that are selected for children through grade 6. The library reminds parents that responsibility for a child's use of library materials, regardless of format or content, lies with the parent or guardian, not the library.

Parents, guardians, teachers, and other caregivers are responsible for the safety and behavior of their children in the Library, and may not leave children under the age of 8 unattended. Children under the age of 8 must be supervised by someone aged 15 or older. Children between the ages of 8 and 12 may be left unattended for up to 2 hours, at the discretion of their parent(s), to complete homework assignments or special projects. These unattended children must know how to reach their parent(s) or guardian, and their parents should pick them up at least 15 minutes prior to the library's scheduled closing time.

If the Library is closing and the parent(s) of children under the age of 12 cannot be located, staff will make a reasonable attempt to contact the parent(s) by phone. For the child's protection, if parent(s) cannot be reached, staff will call the Lexington Police. Staff will wait at the rear entrance with the child until the Police arrive. It is the policy of the Library that staff members may not transport children from the Library to any other location.

If children exhibit disruptive behavior, staff will talk with the child about appropriate modifications. If the behavior persists, parents may be contacted. Some examples of disruptive behavior include: running, shouting, screaming, throwing objects, jumping on the furniture, banging on the fish tank glass, or banging on the computer keyboards. While very uncommon, families with children who resist repeated attempts from staff and parents to modify behavior may be asked to leave and try coming back another day.

Beverages in covered containers are permitted in the Children's Room. Food is limited to the South Lobby, and to approved events in the Meeting Room and Learning Center.

Diaper changing must be restricted to the restroom diaper changing tables, located in every Library restroom. Please place soiled diapers in plastic bags before placing them in the trash. The Children's Room can supply plastic bags, if needed.

Policy approved by the Library Board of Trustees—10.17.12

BEHAVIOR POLICIES/RULES OF CONDUCT: JOPLIN PUBLIC LIBRARY—MISSOURI "LIBRARY RULES FOR PATRONS"

1. The Library is a violence-free facility. Library staff will report to the appropriate authority patron behavior which endangers or threatens another person.
2. Smoking or other use of tobacco products is not allowed in the building.
3. Patrons are not allowed to consume food in the building.
4. Pre-school children must be accompanied by an adult at all times.
5. Use of roller blades, skates, skateboards or scooters is not permitted on Library property.
6. Bathing or doing laundry in the public restrooms is not permitted.
7. Loitering and soliciting on Library property are not allowed.
8. Patrons may not bring pets into the building. Guide dogs or other assistance animals are welcome.

9. Sleeping in the building is not permitted.
10. Patrons may not behave in a disruptive manner or allow their children to behave in a disruptive manner.
11. Patrons may not harass Library personnel or other Library users.
12. Patrons under the influence of drugs or alcohol are not permitted in the building.
13. Shirts and shoes are required.
14. Patrons may not enter the library if they have neglected their bodily hygiene so that it gives offense and constitutes a nuisance to other patrons.
15. Patrons are not permitted to place feet on tables or chairs.
16. Knives, firearms, or other weapons are not permitted.
17. The Library staff assumes no responsibility for unattended children at closing time. The staff will not stay with unattended children or offer transportation home. If an unattended child is in the Library at closing time, the police will be notified and asked to pick up the child.
18. The following behavior may result in criminal prosecution:

    a. Loud, abusive, aggressive, threatening or obscene language or behavior (Disorderly Conduct)
    b. Destroying or damaging Library materials, furniture, or other property (Criminal Mischief)
    c. Using or distributing drugs (Criminal Possession of a Controlled Substance)
    d. Circumventing or attempting to circumvent the Library security system (Petty or Grand Larceny)
    e. Tampering with, altering, editing, or damaging computer hardware and/or software (Computer Related Offenses)

BEHAVIOR POLICIES/RULES OF CONDUCT: MOUNT LEBANON PUBLIC LIBRARY—PITTSBURG, PENNSYLVANIA "PATRON BEHAVIOR POLICY"

POLICY NUMBER: 28
TITLE: Patron Behavior Policy
DATE ISSUED: January 15, 2004
PURPOSE: To protect the rights of individuals who are in the Library to use materials or services, to assist staff members in conducting Library business efficiently, and to preserve Library materials and facilities.

References:

1. The PA Library Code, Act of June 14, 1961, P.L. 324 as amended, particularly sections 415, 426, 427
2. Library policies: Meeting Room #13; Non-Smoking designation #12; Public notice Bulletin Boards #18; Solicitation and Sales #22; Unattended Child #23; Computer Use and Internet Access #24
3. Previously established Library procedures (2001–2003)

D. Statement of Policy:

Library patrons are expected to use the Library, including its facilities, grounds, resources and materials, in a responsible, appropriate, and courteous manner. Illegal acts or conduct in violation of Federal, State, or local laws, ordinances or regulations are prohibited. Behavior that disturbs or infringes on the rights of other Library patrons and staff and which damages library materials and property is not permitted. This policy applies to patrons of all ages.

2. Rules and Regulations:

2.1.   Actions prohibited include, but are not limited to:

2.1.1.   Engaging in disorderly conduct, drunken, dangerous or threatening behavior, fighting or challenging to fight, running, or using offensive words which disturb or tend to disturb the peace or good order of the Library, and any other behavior that is disruptive to Library use.

2.1.2.   Blocking entryways, vestibules, book returns, restrooms, staircases, elevator, or other common areas.

2.1.3.   Refusing to comply with requests of any member of the Library staff to comply with Library policies.

2.1.4.   Using offensive or abusive language or acting or behaving disrespectfully toward a Library employee, volunteer, or patron.

2.1.5.   Any forms of harassment—physical, sexual, verbal—of Library patrons or staff. Harassment may include initiating unwanted conversations, impeding access to the building, stalking, and the like.

2.1.6.   Displaying obscene or sexually explicit materials or Internet sites in violation of 18 Pa. Cons. Stat. Sec 5903. (See also Library policy #24.)

2.1.7.   Excessive noise and other disturbances, such as loud conversation, laughter, cell phone use, or music which is disturbing to others, separate from an authorized library program.

2.1.8.   Selling and/or soliciting for services, money, items, or signatures, except for library or library-related activities. Nothing in this policy shall prohibit a person's freedom of expression of his first amendment rights as guaranteed by the United States Constitution. (See also Library policy #22.)

2.1.9.   Distributing or posting printed materials, literature, or other items that have not been approved by the Library for use inside the Library building. (see also Library policy #18.)

2.1.10.   Possessing or consuming alcohol or illegal drugs or being under the influence of alcohol or drugs.

2.1.11.   Smoking or other uses of tobacco. (see also Library policy #12.)

2.1.12.   Consuming food or beverages in any type container or bringing in packaged or unpackaged food or beverages.

2.1.13.   Not wearing shoes or shirts.

2.1.14.   Bringing animals or pets into the Library (except for assistance animals or for specific Library programs).

2.1.15.   Intentionally damaging, destroying, or stealing any property belonging to the Library or a patron or employee.

2.1.16.   Removing Library materials from the premise without authorization through established lending procedures.

2.1.17.   Using cell phones in the Library. The use of cell phones by patrons is restricted to the entry vestibules of the Library building or outdoors. Cell phones and beepers must be turned off at all times within the library if such device makes an audible sound.

2.1.18.   Moving tables, chairs or other furniture, beyond ordinary use, without permission of Library staff.

2.1.19.   Leaving a child under 8 years of age unattended by a responsible person. (See also Library policy #23.)

2.1.20.   Misuse of restrooms. Restrooms are for the use of Library patrons and staff only. Smoking, changing of clothes, bathing, and hair-washing are not allowed.

2.1.21.   Possessing weapons of any type.

2.1.22.   Indecent exposure.

2.1.23.   Gambling.

2.1.24.   Entering "staff only" areas without permission of Library staff

2.1.25.   Abuse of borrowing privileges.

2.2.   Other: The Library reserves the right to

2.2.1.   Inspect all backpacks, bookbags, satchels, and briefcases. (See 2.1.14 above.)

2.2.2.   Confiscate and dispose of any food, beverage, or containers thereof brought into the Library.

2.2.3.   Limit the number of persons who may sit together at a single table or carrel, in an arrangement of casual seating, or in a study room.

2.2.4.   Separate members of a group from one another or relocate individual from one area of the library to another.

2.2.5.   Impose time limits on the continuous use of library resources, including Reference materials, computer equipment, and public telephones.

2.2.6.   Require patrons to furnish commonly accepted forms of identification, such as driver's licenses and student ID cards

2.3.   The Library is not responsible for personal belongings left unattended. Personal items left by patrons are subject to disposal.

3. Noncompliance:

3.1.   Failure to comply with this policy and/or the Library's established rules, regulations, and procedures will result in a warning and may also result in exclusion from the Library for the day or specified period of time or permanently, and/or in arrest.

3.2.   Theft or damage of Library materials is a serious offense and will result in permanent exclusion from the Library and/or in arrest (PA Law . . . Sec. 427.).

3.3.   Communication of threats, physical violence or sexual offenses will result in permanent exclusion and/or arrest.

3.4.   Trespassers will be arrested and prosecuted.

3.5.   Any person who is asked to leave the Library as a result of the violation of these guidelines and refuses to do so shall be considered to be trespassing. The Library staff will contact the Mt. Lebanon Police Department in all such cases.

3.6.   The Library staff will call the Mt. Lebanon police Department at times when staff deems this to be necessary or prudent.

3.7.   Any patron whose privileges have been denied by Library staff may appeal the decision to the Mt. Lebanon Public Library Board of Trustees within thirty (30) days of the decision.

Please note: Library staff will report unlawful activities to the local police department.

PURPOSE: To provide guidelines to staff for determining inappropriate patron behavior.

POLICY: The Stockton-San Joaquin County Public Library (SSJCPL) has an obligation to its patrons and staff to maintain an atmosphere conducive to reading, study, research, and the pursuit of life-long learning opportunities. Library patrons are expected to use the Library's facilities, resources, and materials in a responsible, appropriate, and courteous way to sustain this environment.

Patrons who fail to follow the Library's behavior guidelines will be subject to appropriate action, which could include expulsion from the Library, the loss of Library privileges, and/or legal action.

GUIDELINES: A. BEHAVIORS WITH PROGRESSIVE CONSEQUENCES

The following examples of unacceptable behavior in Library facilities may result in the patron being banned from all SSJCPL facilities for a specified period of time. This list is for illustrative purposes only and is not meant to be comprehensive; determination of unacceptable behavior is solely at the discretion of Library staff.

1. Refusing to follow the reasonable directions of Library staff.
2. Producing excessive noise.
3. Engaging in behavior that a reasonable person would find to be disruptive or harassing in nature to patrons or Library staff.

4. Consuming food, beverages, or tobacco products outside of designated areas where such use is permitted.
5. Loitering.
6. Soliciting donations of money or anything of value; selling materials or services.
7. Leaving a child 10 years of age or younger unattended in the Library.

B. ZERO TOLERANCE BEHAVIORS

The following examples of unacceptable behavior describe behavior for which there is zero tolerance in SSJCPL facilities. Zero tolerance behaviors will result in an immediate expulsion from all SSJPCL facilities, and the possible long term revocation of Library privileges. This list is for illustrative purposes only; determination of zero tolerance behavior is solely at the discretion of Library staff.

1. Committing or attempting to commit any activity that would constitute a crime or a violation of City or County code.
2. Possession of a weapon or threatening the use of any object in such a manner that it may be considered a weapon.
3. Verbal, physical, written, or electronic harassment or abuse that a reasonable person would consider a potential or real threat to their safety or that of another.
4. Possessing, consuming, or being under the influence of alcohol or narcotics anywhere on Library property.
5. Stealing, damaging, or altering any Library property.
6. Engaging in any sexual contact, activities, or conduct.
7. Displaying child pornography or matter potentially harmful to minors.

C. BEHAVIOR POLICY INFRACTION DISCIPLINE GUIDELINES

In the event that a Library patron engages in behavior that violates the Library Behavior Policy, the patron may be banned from all the Libraries in the system for various periods of time. This document provides *guidelines* for the amount of time that a patron could be banned. Library staff may impose different timelines as warranted.

PROGRESSIVE DISCIPLINE

First infraction:	2 Weeks
Second infraction:	4 Weeks
Third infraction:	2 Months
Fourth infraction:	1 Year
Fifth infraction:	As determined by Library Administration

ZERO TOLERANCE

First infraction—Immediate expulsion and revocation of Library privileges. City of Stockton Library Administration will determine if and when Library privileges will be reinstated.

Date
Name
Street
Anytown, CA, zip code

Dear:

Effective today, you are prohibited from entering any branch of the Stockton-San Joaquin County Public Library until XXXX.

On XXXX, you were observed violating the Library's Behavior Policy by XXXXX. This behavior is unacceptable and interferes with the safe and proper functioning of the Library. Therefore, you are banned from entering any branch or grounds for XXXXX. If you engage in this or other unacceptable behavior after you are allowed to return to the Library, additional restrictions will be placed on your access to the library. If you return to any Library facility or contact the Library through any official Library mode of communication other than the phone number listed below (e.g. telephone, email, social media, etc.) prior to the completion of your banning period, your active banning period may be lengthened at the discretion of Library Administration.

If you have any questions, please contact Library Administration at 209-937-8362.

Sincerely,

Chris Freeman
City Librarian
CF:PE:pe

- Purpose: To establish procedures for handling unattended children in the Library.
- Policy: The Stockton-San Joaquin Public Library is committed to providing a safe and welcoming service environment for all library customers. However, the Library is not a childcare facility; therefore the responsibility for the care, safety and behavior of children in the Library ultimately resides with the parent, legal guardian or other designated responsible caregiver.
- In order to meet this commitment, and because the library is a public building open to anyone, for the safety of all library customers and especially minor children, the following policy has been established to protect the rights and safety of all library customers while on library premises:

  A. All children age ten (10) or younger shall, AT ALL TIMES, be attended and adequately supervised by a responsible person (i.e., a parent, guardian, or other responsible caregiver age 14 or older) and may not be left unattended and/or unsupervised for any amount of time in any area of the library.

  B. Child age ten (10) or younger attending a library program must be brought into the building by a parent, guardian, or other responsible caregiver who must remain in the building until the conclusion of the program when they again resume supervision of their child.

  C. Parents, guardians, or other responsible caregivers are responsible for children's behavior in the library whether or not the parent, guardian or other responsible caregiver is present.

  D. It is not the function of the library to deal with disruptive children. Any child deemed out of control by library staff will be asked to leave for the day after one (1) warning.

  E. The library assumes no responsibility for children left unattended and/or unsupervised on the premises. If children ages 10 and under are found unattended and/or unsupervised in the library, the following actions shall be taken:

     1. A staff member will page the parent/guardian/caregiver and hand them a copy of the Unattended Child Policy and the Library Behavior Policy.
     2. If the parent/guardian/caregiver is not in the building, they will be called on the phone, notified to pick up the unattended/unsupervised child, and given copies of the policies in #1 above.
     3. If the parent/guardian/caregiver cannot be reached or fails to respond, local authorities shall be notified and provided copies of the policies in #1 above to give to the parent/guardian/caregiver.

  F. Consequences:

     1. First infraction: Parent/guardian/caregiver receives copy of policies with explanation of enforcement as indicated above.
     2. Second infraction: Parent/guardian/caregiver's library privileges suspended based on Library Behavior Policy (700-13).

  G. Children age 11 and older may use the library unsupervised. However, they must adhere to all library polices regarding behavior. Children behaving inappropriately may be given a warning and/or asked to leave the library at the discretion of library staff. If asked to leave, library staff shall make all reasonable efforts to contact the child's parent/guardian/

caregiver to have the child picked up. If a parent/guardian/caregiver cannot be reached and/or fails to respond within 15 minutes of the library closing, staff shall contact local authorities. The child shall remain in the library with staff until either a parent/guardian/caretaker or authorities arrive. Upon arrival, the parent/guardian/caregiver (or authority) shall be handed a copy of the unattended child policy.

APPENDIX E

CIVIL DISORDER AND DEMONSTRATIONS/TERRORISM
CHILLICOTHE PUBLIC LIBRARY—ILLINOIS

Notify authorities immediately of any information received, factual or rumored, of a demonstration or other form of civil disorder, which is planned, or in progress in the vicinity of the library.

Follow the instructions of supervisor and other emergency personnel. Assist with protecting objects.

If an explosion occurs, take cover immediately and anticipate there may be others.

Notify authorities of any potential/actual hazards (e.g., fire bomb threat), incurred during a threatening situation.

Press one of the three "Panic Buttons" located under the middle, front edge of any of the three service desks if unable to use the telephone.

Stay indoors and away from windows unless directed to evacuate by emergency preparedness personnel.

Evacuate when directed and follow evacuation procedures.

Assemble in the Southeast corner of the parking lot, across from the flagpole, unless directed to do otherwise.

APPENDIX F

REFERRALS TO OUTSIDE AGENCIES
VELMA TEAGUE BRANCH LIBRARY—GLENDALE, ARIZONA
"WHEN YOU NEED A LITTLE HELP . . ."

(Note: These are the categories in the Velma Teague Branch's brochure, "When You Need a Little Help." Fill them in with your own local resources and their phone numbers and addresses.)

Nutritional Needs

Food Hotline
Applying for Food Stamps
Food Pantries
Food Banks
Salvation Army

Shelters

Domestic Violence Shelters
Family Advocacy Centers

Medical Care

Family Health Centers
Free Clinics
County Clinics

Community Action Programs

Utility payment
Utility deposit
Mortgage payment to prevent eviction/foreclosure
Rent to prevent eviction
First month's rent for those who are homeless
Rental deposit for those who are homeless
Home weatherization
Repair/replacement of utility related appliances

APPENDIX G

MATERIALS CHALLENGE FORM
JOPLIN, MISSOURI PUBLIC LIBRARY
"COMMENT ON LIBRARY MATERIALS FORM"

Title _____ Author

_____ Book Periodical Videotape/DVD

Audiobook Other _____ Publisher

_____ Copyright Date

_____ Call Number

Comment initiated by _____ Library Card

Number _____ Address

_____

_____ City _____ State _____

Zip _____ Telephone _____ Do you represent:

_____ Yourself

_____ An Organization (name) _____

_____ Another group (name) _____

To what in the work do you object? Please be specific. Cite page numbers
of book or scene, etc., of film or audio.

_____

What were the circumstances under which this work came to your
attention? _____

_____

Did you read/view/listen to the entire work? If not, what part(s) did you
read/view/listen to?

_____

What do you believe is the theme of this work?

_____

_____

From *Crash Course in Dealing with Difficult Library Customers* by Shelley E. Mosley, Dennis C. Tucker, and Sandra
Van Winkle. Santa Barbara, CA: Libraries Unlimited. Copyright © 2014.

Have you read or are you aware of judgments of this work by literary
critics and/or professional reviewers?

_____

For what age group would you recommend this work?

_____

Do you feel there are library patrons who would not object to this work?

_____

Have you read the selection policy of the Joplin Public Library?
_____ Of which part of the selection
policy do you feel this work is in violation?

_____

_____ Signature

Date

APPENDIX H

MATERIALS COMPLAINT POLICIES AND FORMS: CHILLICOTHE PUBLIC LIBRARY—ILLINOIS "REQUEST FOR RECONSIDERATION OF LIBRARY MATERIAL"

Author/Composer/Perform_____

Title_____

Hardcover _____

Paperback_____ Film_____ Recording_____

Periodical_____

Pamphlet_____ Other _____

Request initiated by _____

Address_____ Phone_____

City_____ Zip Code_____

Citizen represents:

Self_____

Organization_____ Name_____

Other_____ Name_____

Are you familiar with the Alliance Library System's materials selection policy, the
ALA Library Bill of Rights, the Freedom to Read, and the Freedom to View
statements?

_____YES _____NO

Did you read/hear/view the entire work?_____
_____

If not, what parts?_____
_____

What portion of the material do you wish reconsidered? (Please be specific, cite
pages, record side, band number, etc.)
_____
_____

Why do you wish it to be reconsidered?
_____
_____ D-10

What are the worthwhile aspects of this work?

_____

_____

What would you like the library system to do with this material?

_____

_____

_____

Can you recommend materials that would convey the same values and perspective of our society that the system could consider for purchase?

_____

_____

_____

_____

_____

DATE   SIGNATURE

APPENDIX I

LAWS REGARDING LIBRARY VANDALISM MASSACHUSETTS

Part IV Crimes, Punishments and Proceedings In Criminal Cases Title I Crimes And Punishments

Chapter 266 Crimes Against Property

§ 100. Library Related Crimes—Defacement of Library Materials; Restitution; Penalty.

Whoever willfully, maliciously or wantonly writes upon, injures, defaces, tears, cuts, mutilates or destroys any library material or property, shall make restitution in full replacement value of the library materials or property, and, in addition, shall be punished by imprisonment in a house of correction for not more than two years or by a fine of not less than one hundred nor more than one thousand dollars, or both.

A law enforcement officer may arrest without warrant any person he has probable cause to believe has violated the provisions of section ninety-nine A and this section. The statement of an employee or agent of the library, eighteen years of age or older, that a person has violated the provisions of said section ninety-nine A and this section shall constitute probable cause for arrest by a law enforcement officer authorized to make an arrest in such jurisdiction. The activation of an electronic anti-theft device shall constitute probable cause for believing that a person has violated the provisions of this section.

A library shall prepare posters to be displayed therein in a conspicuous place. Said posters shall contain a summary and explanation of said section ninety-nine A and this section.

LAWS REGARDING LIBRARY VANDALISM: CALIFORNIA OFFENSES AGAINST LIBRARIES

(Education Code Title 1, Division 1, Part 11, Chapter 11, Article 2, Sections 19910–19911; Penal Code Section 490.5 and 11413.)

Sec. 19910. Malicious damage

Any person who maliciously cuts, tears, defaces, breaks, or injures any book, map, chart, picture, engraving, statue, coin, model, apparatus, or other work of literature, art, mechanics, or object of curiosity, deposited in any public library, gallery, museum, collection, fair, or exhibition, is guilty of a misdemeanor.

The parent or guardian of a minor who willfully and maliciously commits any act within the scope of this section shall be liable for all damages so caused by the minor.

Sec. 19911. Willful detention of property

Any person who willfully detains any book, newspaper, magazine, pamphlet, manuscript, or other property belonging to any public or incorporated library, reading room, museum, or other educational institution, for 30 days after notice in writing to return the article or property, given after the expiration of the time for which by the rules of the institution the article or property may be kept, is guilty of a misdemeanor.

The parent or guardian of a minor who willfully and maliciously commits any act within the scope of this section shall be liable for all damages so caused by the minor.

APPENDIX J

LAWS REGARDING LIBRARY THEFT
OKLAHOMA STATUTES

Oklahoma Statutes Title 21. Crimes and Punishments

Chapter 68—Larceny Section 1739—Library Theft

A. As used in this section:

1. "Library facility" means any:

    a. public library; or
    b. library of an educational, historical or eleemosynary institution, organization, or society; or
    c. museum; or
    d. repository of public or institutional records.

2. "Library material" means any book, plate, picture, photograph, engraving, painting, drawing, map, newspaper, magazine, pamphlet, broadside, manuscript, document, letter, record, microform, sound recording, audiovisual materials in any format, magnetic or other tapes, catalog cards or catalog records, electronic data processing records, computer software, artifacts, or other documentary, written or printed materials regardless of physical form or characteristics, belonging or on loan to, or otherwise in the custody of a library facility.

3. "Demand" means either actual notice to the possessor of any library materials or the mailing of written notice to the possessor at the last address of record which the library facility has for said person, demanding the return of designated library materials. If demand is made by mail it shall be deemed to have been given as of the date the notice is mailed by the library facility.

B. Any person shall be guilty, upon conviction, of library theft who willfully:

1. Removes or attempts to remove any library material from the premises of a library facility without authority; or
2. Mutilates, destroys, alters or otherwise damages, in whole or in part, any library materials; or
3. Fails to return any library materials which have been lent to said person by the library facility, within seven (7) days after demand has been made for the return of the library materials.

C. A person convicted of library theft shall be guilty of a misdemeanor and shall be subject to the fine and restitution provisions of this subsection but shall not be subject to imprisonment. The punishment for conviction of library theft shall be:

1. If the aggregate value of the library material is Five Hundred Dollars ($500.00) or less, by fine not exceeding One Thousand Dollars ($1,000.00), or the offender shall make restitution to the library facility, including payment of all related expenses incurred by the library facility as a result of the actions of the offender, or both such fine and restitution; or

2. If the aggregate value of the library material is greater than Five Hundred Dollars ($500.00), by fine not exceeding Ten Thousand Dollars ($10,000.00), or the offender shall make restitution to the library facility, including payment of all expenses incurred by the library facility as a result of the actions of the offender, or both such fine and restitution.

D. Copies of the provisions of this section shall be posted on the premises of each library facility.

APPENDIX K

BODY FLUIDS/HAZMAT CHILLICOTHE PUBLIC LIBRARY—ILLINOIS BODY FLUIDS/HAZMAT

Bodily Fluids

Spill Clean-Up Packs for the removal and cleaning of body fluid spills are located in the third drawer down on the right-hand side of the circulation desk. This drawer is indicated by a red, sticky dot on the front.

Procedure for handling a bodily fluid spill:

- Always wear gloves when potentially infectious fluids are present. Do not use gloves if torn or punctured. Shake powder from kit directly onto the spill.

Allow five minutes to congeal.

Use the scoop and spatula provided in the kit to pick up gelled material.

Disinfect area with cloth.

Procedure for disposal:

For spills involving blood or other potentially infectious fluids, use the biohazard bag provide in the kit. Dispose of bag in accordance with local regulations.

Bloodborne Pathogens Policy

1. While normal library operation are not likely to involve circumstances exposing employees or users to bloodborne pathogens, the Chillicothe Public Library District complies with Illinois Department of Labor regulations to occupational exposures to bloodborne pathogens which have been incorporated by administrative actions.
2. Exposure Determination: No particular job classification of the Library has occupation exposure (meaning "reasonably anticipated . . . contact with blood or other potentially infectious materials that may result from the performance of an employee's duties"), however, emergencies may occur with staff or patrons, particularly youth or elderly patrons, to which library employees in all classifications may be called upon to respond with assistance. Or emergencies with "out of control" individuals (e.g. biting, spitting, etc.) could present an individual threat.

3. Universal Precautions: All potential circumstances of exposures must be taken into account by the Library and its employees to protect against exposures. Hepatitis B (HBV), human immunodeficiency virus (HI), and other bloodborne pathogens found in human blood and other body fluids cause life-threatening diseases. In emergency or other such circumstances, when contact with blood or other potentially infectious materials may result, the Library's approach to infection control requires all human blood and body fluids to be treated as if known to be infectious for HIV, HBV, and other bloodborne pathogens. Engineering and work practice controls shall be used to eliminate or minimize employee exposures, and if a possibility of exposure remains, personal protective equipment shall also be used.

4. Exposure Control Plan: At any time within the Library environment that human blood, human body fluids, or other potentially infectious material are presented, the area contaminated shall be immediately cordoned off and quarantined, even if the entire library must be closed to accomplish this completely. Personal protection clothing, such as gloves, gowns, masks, etc., shall be provided and used in the cleanup and safe disposal of contaminated waste such as diapers, blood-tinged material (e.g. Band-Aids, gauze, cotton, clothing, etc.) etc. if advisable, a professional hazardous/contaminated cleanup firm shall be proved by the Library and must be used by the employees as soon as feasible, including following the removal of personal protective equipment. A complete record of all incidents, exposures, cleanup, and disposals shall be kept as required by the regulations.

5. Training Immunizations: The Library shall provide directly or through System, State, or associational programs, annual in-service training/educations programs for affected employees. Any employee who has occupational exposures shall be offered, at no charge, the hepatitis B vaccine series, in accordance with the regulations. Following the report of an exposure incident, the Library will make immediately available to the exposed employee or employees a confidential medical evaluation and follow-up as provided in the regulations.

APPENDIX L

FIRE SAFETY PROCEDURES
CHILLICOTHE PUBLIC LIBRARY—ILLINOIS "FIRE"

Remain calm.

Contact the Fire Department using 911.

If the fire is small, try to extinguish it with the proper type of extinguisher or other method. When using the fire extinguisher, remember PASS—Pull, Aim, Squeeze and Sweep.

Do not jeopardize personal safety.

Do not allow the fire to come between you and the exit.

Disconnect electrical equipment if it is on fire and it is safe to do so.

Notify your supervisor, if possible.

Evacuate if you cannot extinguish the fire. Assist disabled persons if possible.

Follow the fire instructions on the "Escape Route" signs located next to the doorways in each room of the library.

Do not break windows unless that is the only way out.

Stay low to the ground when escaping a smoke filled room.

Do not open a hot door. Before opening a door, touch it near the top with the back of your hand. If it is hot or if smoke is visible, DO NOT OPEN.

After escaping, close doors in each room to delay the spread of the fire.

Learn to stop, drop to the ground, and roll if clothes catch fire.

If possible, cover mouth with a cloth to avoid inhaling smoke and gases.

Do not attempt to save possessions.

Go directly to the Southeast corner of the parking lot, across from the flagpole.

Do not return to the building until told to by appropriate authorities.

FIRE SAFETY PROCEDURES:
JOPLIN, MISSOURI PUBLIC LIBRARY
"FIRE ALARM PROCEDURES"

Fire alarms must be treated with the utmost seriousness. All Library staff are responsible for knowing departmental and individual responsibilities in case of a fire alarm.

A. ASSIGNED RESPONSIBILITIES

1. The Circulation Desk is responsible for checking the box in the west vestibule, the alarm across from the women's bathroom, and the alarm at the check-in station.
2. Technical Services is responsible for checking the alarm by the back door and the alarm in the large meeting room.
3. The Post Library is responsible for checking the alarm at the Post Library entrance.
4. Reference is responsible for checking the alarm by the south fire exit.
5. The Administrative staff is responsible for checking the penthouse and remaining in the maintenance area until the alarm is silenced.
6. If an alarm sounds on a weekend or evening or at any time when either Technical Services or the Post Library is unstaffed, the Circulation Desk is responsible for checking all alarms at the north end of the building and Reference is responsible for checking all alarms at the south end of the building.
7. If the building must be evacuated, staff members must make sure that all patrons leave the building. All departments are responsible for clearing their own areas, and Circulation Desk staff will assist Reference in clearing the stacks. Patrons in the stack area and Computer Lab should leave by the south fire door.
8. One staff member must remain at the Circulation Desk by the phone until all patrons are out of the building.
9. Keys for the alarms should be visibly marked and easily accessible. Every staff member must know where the keys are located. The children's department alarm box does not have a key. Children's staff must follow the instructions on the pull box located across from the Children's Desk.
10. The alarm must not be silenced until the Circulation Desk is notified that:

    1. An alarm box was pulled in error
    2. It is evident that there is no fire.

11. Upon notification from the Circulation Desk, the Library Director will silence the alarm. In the Director's absence, a Department Head will silence the alarm. If no Department Heads are on duty, the Circulation Desk staff will silence the alarm.

B. PROCEDURES CHECKLIST IN THE CASE OF A FIRE ALARM

1) Determine if there is a fire.
2) If the panel in the west vestibule says there is a fire in the penthouse, it may be smoke, perhaps from outside, in the air handlers. The fire department can check this out. Meanwhile, patrons and staff must be evacuated.
3) The alarm must remain on until the building is cleared.
4) Staff members must check each pull station to see if one has been pulled. If a station has been pulled in error, the staff member will reset the station as follows:

    a) Insert and turn key and open door. (Children's department follow instructions on pull box.)
    b) Close door and relock.

5) If the alarm goes off again, another pull station is still pulled.

benefits or other portions of this manual at any time, or from time to time, with or without notice.

All policies reviewed and approved by the Joplin Public Board of Trustees on 13 November 2006. Changes, additions, deletions, etc. to individual sections will be dated individually as amended.

6) The Circulation Desk can silence the alarm with key in the west vestibule or go to the Mechanical Control room behind the custodian's office and:

   a) Locate the red Simplex box and open it
   b) Press ACK button on upper left side. This will silence the alarm.
   c) After the pull station has been located and reset, press the button below ACK button to reset the alarm system. This will make a terrible noise.
   d) Flip the SILENCE toggle switch to silence the noise.

7) Once it has been determined that there is no fire and that all is safe, call the fire department to cancel the alarm. It is probable that the fire department will already be on the scene.

APPENDIX M

BOMB THREATS CHILLICOTHE PUBLIC LIBRARY— ILLINOIS "BOMB THREAT"

Remain calm.

Press the panic button located under the front edge in the middle of each of the libraries service desks while staying on the phone.

Listen carefully. Listen for any background noises that could give a clue to caller's location.

Listen closely to the voice (male or female), voice quality (calm or excited), and accent and speech impediments. Be polite and show interest.

Try to keep the caller talking to learn more information, i.e., type of bomb, location of the bomb and when it will be detonated.

Do not hang up the phone that the call was received on, even after the caller hangs up. Sometimes the caller can be traced.

If possible, write a note to a colleague to call the authorities or, as soon as the caller hangs up, immediately notify them. Survey work area for unusual packages in unusual places. If anything looks strange, do not touch it. Make a quick visual study of the size and location of the area.

DO NOT TOUCH!

Write down as much detail as you can remember.

Do not discuss the threat with other staff. If there is time, tell employees to unlock desks, lockers and file cabinets and turn off machinery before they leave the office.

If time allows, open windows and doors to minimize blast and fragmentation damage.

Follow instructions of emergency preparedness personnel.

Evacuate when directed and assemble at the Southeast corner of the parking lot across from the flagpole.

SUSPICIOUS MAIL

If you receive a suspicious letter or package: Handle with care. Don't shake or bump. Isolate it immediately

Don't open, smell, touch or taste

Treat it as suspect. Call local law enforcement authorities.

Things to look for on letters or packages:

No return address and/or restrictive markings
Oily stains, discolorations or crystallization on wrapper or envelope
Excessive tape or string
Rigid or bulky
Strange odor. Do not sniff!
Lopsided or uneven edges.
Misspelled words, addressed to title only, incorrect title or badly typed or written address.
Possibly mailed from foreign country
If a parcel is open and/or a threat is identified:

For a Bomb

Evacuate immediately.
Call the police, or press one of the "Panic Buttons" located in the middle under the front edge of all three service desks. Contact postal inspectors.
Call local fire department/Hazardous Materials unit at 911.

For Radiological

Limit exposure—don't handle
Evacuate area
Shield yourself from object
Call the police, or press one of the "Panic Buttons" located in the middle under the front edge of all three service desks Contact postal inspectors.
Call local fire department/HAZMAT unit.

For Biological or Chemical

Isolate—don't handle.
Evacuate immediate area.
Wash your hands with soap and warm water.
Call the police, or press one of the "Panic Buttons" located in the middle under the front edge of all three service desks Contact postal inspectors
Call the local fire department/HAZMAT unit.

EXPLOSION

Remain calm.
Take cover under a table or desk.
Be prepared for possible further explosions.
Stay away from windows, mirrors, overhead fixtures, filing cabinets, bookcases, and shelving.
Evacuate calmly, when directed, to the assembly area located in the Southeast corner of the parking lot across from the flagpole.
Do not move seriously injured persons unless they are in immediate danger (e.g. fire, building collapse, etc.).
Open doors carefully.
Watch for falling objects.
Avoid using the telephone, except in a life threatening situation.
Do not use matches or lighters.

Contact emergency personnel by use of cell phones if possible.

Do not reenter the affected area until directed to do so by supervisor or emergency personnel.

BOMB THREATS JOPLIN, MISSOURI PUBLIC LIBRARY "BOMB THREATS"

A. Introduction and Purpose

The Joplin Public Library is considered at risk to bomb threats but is judged to be at no greater a risk than other jurisdictions with a similar purpose or demographics. Since this risk factor cannot be fully mitigated, plans must be developed to deal with the risk and people must be trained to respond to any such risk. This procedure is designed to establish responsibilities and expectations relative to the handling of bomb threats against Joplin Public Library employees, patrons, visitors and facilities.

B. Responsibility

1. It will be the responsibility of each Department Head to ensure employees are properly trained in bomb threat procedures. The City of Joplin Emergency Management Director will provide information and assistance to Library Department Heads if such assistance is requested.

2. A new employee of the Library will receive an orientation of the bomb threat procedures from his or her Department Head within the first week of employment. The orientation will address the following areas as a minimum:

   1. Filling out the bomb threat check list card.
   2. Who to contact after receipt of a bomb threat call.
   3. Search procedures.
   4. Evacuation procedures.

C. Bomb Threats

1. The possibility of two types of bombing scenarios exists—terrorist bombing and bomb threat.

1. Terrorist Bombing. Typically, no warning or advance notification is given. The bomber places an explosive or incendiary device and it explodes, creating havoc and mayhem to everything in the area. In an effort to help safeguard against such actions, employees should report any suspicious situation or circumstance, no matter how insignificant it may seem, to the immediate supervisor. Management personnel must respond to these notifications by at least checking them out and, if circumstances warrant, contacting law enforcement personnel. Library personnel should not take any action except notification.

2. Bomb Threat. There are only two reasonable explanations for bomb threats.

   (1) The caller has definite knowledge that an explosive device has been placed and wants to minimize personal injury or property damage. The caller may be the person who placed the device or someone who has become aware of such information.

   (2) The caller wants to create an atmosphere of anxiety and panic which will, in turn, possibly result in a disruption of normal activities for the facility where the device has purportedly been placed. The caller may have a political, economic or social agenda. An important consolation regarding bomb threats is that the vast majority are hoaxes. However, it is impossible to know immediately whether a bomb threat is real.

If a Written Threat is Received:

- Save all materials.
- Protect evidence.
- Notify supervisor and immediately contact the Emergency Communications Center at 9-1-1.

If a Threat is Received by Telephone:

- Do not panic. The goal of the caller is to create panic.
- Utilize the Bomb Threat Card placed near your phone. Information obtained by the call recipient helps determine the validity of a threat. In most hoax calls, the caller is vague and general in his or her answers. Conversely, if the caller is specific and detailed in his or her answers, the chances are greater that the threat is real.
- Listen carefully. Note if possible the exact words spoken, sex of the caller, approximate age, speech (slang, accent, impediment,) behavior (calm, nervous, scared,) background noises, etc.
- At the conclusion of the call, the recipient should immediately call 9-1-1 and report the threat.
- The Communications Center will notify the Police and Fire Departments of the threat.
- If warranted, the Library should be evacuated immediately according to the evacuation procedure outlined in this policy.

Threat Evaluation.

- It is the responsibility of the Joplin Fire/Police Department to determine the degree of validity of the threat based on information received from the caller.
- It is also the responsibility of the Joplin Fire/Police Department to determine the method of response, either Overt (Total Response) or Covert (Controlled Response.)

Covert Response. If the caller states that the bomb is not set to detonate for a while and gives only non-descriptive information, a search of the facility may be initiated prior to the issuance of an evacuation order. Search procedures will be as follows:

- Locate and remove personal items; by removing personal items, employees limit the number of suspect items.
- Pair up for search. Searchers should listen carefully for any unusual noises, such as ticking or humming.
- Select height level for search—first level floor to desk top, second level desk top to ceiling. Searchers should never disturb or look above ceiling tiles.
- Do not close doors or windows or disturb anything.
- Note suspect devices—anything that does not belong, such as a briefcase, lunch box, backpack, sewing box, thermos, camera case, etc.
- If a suspect device is found, do not touch it. It is imperative that searchers understand their purpose is only to search for and report suspicious objects. The removal/disarming of an explosive device must be the responsibility of professionals in explosive ordnance disposal.

Overt Response. If a descriptive bomb threat is received and/or if there is little or no time available to search, the Joplin Fire Department may issue an evacuation order.

APPENDIX N

PROBLEM PATRON POLICY:
BUCKEYE PUBLIC LIBRARY—ARIZONA

"GUIDELINES FOR DEALING WITH PROBLEM BEHAVIOR"

When dealing with problem behavior, staff should keep the following points in mind:

1. Assume that patrons have a legitimate reason for using the library until they exhibit symptoms of problem behavior as defined in this section of the manual.
2. Even though the Library, History and Arts Manager and the Branch Manager have the ultimate responsibility for dealing with this type of behavior, all staff has a degree of responsibility. Reporting a potential problem is very important.
3. Use common sense in dealing with the situation. Listen carefully to the patron. Respond in a calm manner. Try not to panic or become angry. Try to speak normally.
4. Take a firm, realistic position and explain it fully. Do not get into arguments.
5. Do not use physical force. Do not touch the patron.
6. Do not hesitate to call the police, press the panic button, or activate the security alarm in a critical or overwhelming situation.
7. Teamwork is important in dealing with a difficult customer. Reinforcement help may be necessary.
8. Be consistent and fair in enforcing rules. As an example, do not single out one age group.
9. If a patron becomes violent or threatens to do so, leave them and yourself a way out. Do not block an escape route.

PROBLEM PATRON POLICY: CORNING PUBLIC LIBRARY

"DECORUM OF LIBRARY PATRON"

It is expected that the library patron will conduct himself/herself with respect and courtesy to the library staff and other patrons. Observance of library policy and rules is expected at all times. Abuse of library privileges will result in a warning by the head librarian or in his/her absence by the staff member in charge. Continued abuse may result in suspension of some or all library privileges at the discretion of the head librarian.

A patron who feels he/she has been unfairly suspended may file an appeal in writing with the board of trustees. Appeals will be considered at the next regular meeting of the board of trustees, provided they have been received seven days prior to the meeting.

PROBLEM PATRON POLICY: CONRAD PUBLIC LIBRARY

"THE UNRULY OR DISRUPTIVE PATRON"

At the discretion of the librarian, the unruly or disruptive patron may be asked to leave the premises for a specified period of time, or they may lose certain library privileges. If the patron is a minor, a parent will be notified of the disciplinary action.

The Unattended Child

The library does not provide a babysitting service. Preschool children are expected to be accompanied and supervised by a responsible person. Older, unattended children who are disruptive will be dealt with according to the library's stated policy.

PROBLEM PATRON POLICY: GUTHRIE CENTER PUBLIC LIBRARY—GUTHRIE CENTER, IOWA

PROBLEM PATRON POLICY

Introduction

Part of the staff's responsibility is to keep the library a pleasant environment for as many people as possible. In a library as overcrowded as ours is, this isn't always an easy task. Problems arise because, ironically enough, our efforts to create an enjoyable atmosphere sometimes attract people who jeopardize the work we've done.

It is important that we not ignore a patron whose behavior drives others out of the building. It is equally important that we be tolerant of a patron who behaves unusually but doesn't disturb others. These guidelines are designed both to help the staff decide if a patron is really being a problem and to provide ways to deal with problem patrons.

    I. IRATE PATRONS This is a problem we all face when working with the public. First of all, be sure it is not your behavior that is causing the patron to show heated emotions. Be sure that your muscles are relaxed and that you do not come across as being combative or poised for battle. Alternatively, don't appear fearful. A limp, uncaring, or "tough apples" attitude is destructive. You should feel that your job is to obtain for the patron what he/she wants if it is at all possible. If it is not, say you are genuinely regretful but the reasons for the library's inability to comply are good ones. If you feel you are being helpful and the patron is not responding to you in a manner that is respectful, consider calling another staff member to help. It is possible that someone else on the staff will be able to help you.

II. DESTRUCTIVE BEHAVIOR Destructive patrons can be careless or thoughtless; others can be dangerous. You must size up the situation and decide the best method of handling it. If the patron seems harmless, making him or her aware that you know what he or she is doing should be enough to stop the problem. If the patron is obviously not approachable, call assistance and a supervisor to help you. Examples of destructive behavior are listed below:

Destroying or damaging of library material such as books, pamphlets, films, magazines, records, cassettes, art prints.

Destroying or damaging library equipment such as typewriters, copy machines, microfilm readers, stereo equipment, cassette players.

Vandalism of library property. Defacing walls, damaging facilities (such as restrooms), breaking windows.

III. BEHAVIORAL PROBLEMS

    A. Definition

        These problems which are not of a threatening nature but are nonetheless disruptive. They are also the problems which seem to occur most frequently in the library.

        Behavioral problems include: strong smell, noisiness, excessive chattiness with staff or patrons, and other types of obnoxious behavior.

        Other patrons are not always quick to report an obnoxious patron to the staff. The staff should be alert to signs that a patron with a behavioral problem is present. These signs include: patrons moving away from another patron, patrons staring at another patron, patrons looking at staff members as a form of complaint. Sometimes the staff member will notice a problem patron, and other times there may be an actual complaint.

    B. Guidelines

        Noisy adult patrons should be told that their behavior is improper in the library. This advice should be repeated if necessary. If that strategy is unsuccessful, the patron should be told that he or she will have to leave if the behavior continues to be a problem. Finally, the patron should be asked to leave. Staff members should be polite, but firm.

        Chatty patrons are usually lonely people, and the staff should be tolerant of their behavior as long as the noise doesn't disturb others. If a patron's chattiness begins to distract a staff member from helping other patrons, the staff member should politely excuse him or herself and explain that he or she must help another person.

        Smelly persons who are offending others should be asked to leave until they've cleaned themselves. This may be uncomfortable, but we can assume that anyone who smells so strongly knows it and Is intentionally behaving in this manner.

IV. CHILDREN Children can be problem patrons for a variety of reasons. Handling depends on the individual situation.

    A. Noise—Single or small groups should be told in a firm, but nice way, that their behavior is inappropriate in a library and that they are disturbing others. If they repeat actions, remind them in a stricter tone of voice. Larger groups, especially during children's programs (puppet shows, movies, story hours), present a difficult problem. It is almost impossible to control large group situations. If other patrons complain, explain the circumstances and apologize.

B. Running and playing are hazardous and should be stopped at once.

C. Attention seeking or demanding children (e.g. repeated questions; talking to staff), should be discouraged since it disrupts work activity.

D. The use of the library as a temporary baby-sitting service by parents should be discouraged. Tell parents we are not such a service and cannot be responsible for their children.

E. Children can be a problem even with their parents. If they are disturbing others, approach the parent first and inform them of their children's actions. Often, they are so accustomed to their child's behavior that they are not aware of its effects on others. A good thing to say would be, "I'm sorry but your child seems to be disturbing others."

F. Miscellaneous discipline problems are so varied that each situation should be handled as it occurs. If it seems you cannot deal with it, contact a supervisor.

V. SEXUAL DEVIATES You can be sure that what these people are looking for is some sort of shock or surprise reaction.

A. Peekers: This problem happens to staff and public alike. There might be a few suggestions that will discourage this behavior.

The way one dresses and carries oneself will have something to do with this. Pants are good to wear if one has to work out in the stacks shelving.

If someone is watching you, be sure to get a description. BE SURE TO TELL YOUR SUPERVISOR.

Many times if you can confront the individual and let him know that you know what he is up to it will stop him from doing it. Do not let the peeker get the best of you. "Do you need help finding something?", is something you might ask if you confront him. If the problem gets bad, we may want to let another agency in to help us.

B. Flashers: These people are very passive, not violent.

Get a description.

Try not to show alarm as this behavior thrives on it.

Tell supervisors and fellow workers.

Call description into police.

C. This is a serious problem and should not be taken lightly.

VI. MENTALLY DISTURBED

A. Define problem: Decide whether individual is dangerous or not, and whether behavior is bothersome or not.

B. Not Dangerous

Bothersome behavior

Sit down with the patron and attempt to reason.

Do not argue the individual out of hallucinations or delusions.

Have another staff member within viewing distance if you are not certain of the individual's reaction.

Do not corner the individual. Allow him or her space to easily leave the building.

If disturbance continues, firmly tell the person his behavior is inappropriate and that he will have to leave.

If the Individual refuses to leave, get assistance from another staff member or if need be, call the police.

Not bothersome

Ignore unusual behavior if not disturbing others.

C. Dangerous

Notify Librarian or City Clerk

Call police.

    D.   Handling them

Talk in a firm, commanding voice.

Do not touch the patron! (Depersonalization). This is something that often happens—the psychotic will be having a hard time holding themselves together. If you touch them they weird out!!

If they do not respect your command, call police.

Be consistent in how you treat everyone!

Inform you supervisor whenever you've had to deal with a problem patron.

VII. ALCOHOL

    A.   Definition

Anyone carrying a bottle of beer, wine or liquor in the library (including the `rest rooms) should be considered a problem patron.

Judgement should be exercised in the case of people who smell of alcohol. If the patron's behavior is not otherwise offensive, then there's no problem. If, on the other hand, the patron is loud, obnoxious, or in some other way behaving improperly, guideline steps should be followed.

    B.   Guidelines

The staff member who notices a patron who is drunk and drinking in the library should decide whether to handle the problem or request help from other employees. The patron should be asked to leave the library, because "Drinking is inappropriate in a public library."

If the patron refuses or the staff feels the patron is too dangerous to be dealt with, the police should be called. The police will decide whether to take the person or, if the person is violent, the police will arrest him or her.

VIII. DRUGS

    A.   Definition

It is not always obvious whether a person who is acting strangely is under the influence of drugs or suffering from a more permanent psychological problem.

Someone behaving in a particularly bizarre fashion might be assumed to be under the influence of drugs, because people with everyday psychic disorders of such an extreme nature are probably not out on the streets.

    B.   Guidelines

The patron shouldn't be made to feel threatened, as this will only make the situation worse.

IX. WEAPONS

    A.   Definition

Iowa law now states that it is illegal to carry a dangerous weapon in a public building.

According to the police, a knife is not a dangerous weapon, and a gun must be loaded to be considered dangerous.

For our purposes, a knife worn on a patron's belt will be allowed In the library. However, a knife held in a threatening manner is definitely a problem. Any gun in the library will be considered a problem, also.

    B.   Guidelines

Call the police immediately.

Before the police arrive, the staff is responsible for protecting other patrons in the building.

PROBLEM PATRON POLICY:
JOPLIN, MISSOURI PUBLIC LIBRARY

"PATRON PROBLEM BEHAVIOR"

1. If a patron's behavior is abusive, causes problems for other patrons, threatens the safety or well being of patrons or staff, or threatens to cause damage to Library property, any Department Head or other employee may require the offending patron to leave Library property. If a patron refuses to leave, the employee should call law enforcement authorities.

2. If a patron's behavior is such that confrontation with a Library employee might, in the employee's best judgment, result in physical harm to any person or in damage to Library property, the employee should report the situation immediately to any Department Head, who should request assistance from law enforcement authorities. If no Department Head is available, the employee should request assistance from law enforcement authorities. Under no circumstances should employees offer resistance to a patron or attempt to physically restrain or apprehend a patron.

3. Patrons who exhibit a pattern of offensive behavior may be denied access to the Library for a period of time to be determined by the Library Director or his/her designee.

   An employee who observes a patron deliberately attempting to steal, deface, or damage Library property must immediately request police assistance and be prepared to cooperate with law enforcement authorities in pursuing legal action against the patron.

SUGGESTED RESOURCES

Amador, Xavier. *I Am Not Sick, I Don't Need Help! How to Help Someone with Mental Illness Accept Treatment* (10th ed.). New York: Vida, 2011. Print.

American Library Association. *ALA Policy Manual*, "B.3.3 Combating Prejudice, Stereotyping, and Discrimination." Web May 21, 2013. http://www.ala.org/aboutala/sites/ala.org.aboutala/files/content/governance/policymanual/Links/cd_10_2_Section%20B%20New%20Policy%20Manual-1%20(final%204–11–13%20with%20TOC).pdf

American Library Association. *ALA Policy Manual*, Policy "B.3.2 Combating Racism." Web May 21, 2013. http://www.ala.org/aboutala/sites/ala.org.aboutala/files/content/governance/policymanual/Links/cd_10_2_Section%20B%20New%20Policy%20Manual-1%20(final%204–11–13%20with%20TOC).pdf

American Library Association. *ALA Policy Manual*, Policy "B.3 Diversity." Web May 21, 2013. http://www.ala.org/aboutala/governance/policymanual/updatedpolicymanual/section2/diversity

American Library Association. *Intellectual Freedom Manual* (8th ed.). 2010. Print.

American Library Association. "Intellectual Freedom Toolkits." http://www.ala.org/advocacy/intfreedom/iftoolkits/intellectual

American Library Association. "Public Library Use." ALA Library Fact Sheet 6." 2011. Web May 7, 2013. http://www.ala.org/tools/libfactsheets/alalibraryfactsheet06#state

American Psychological Association. "Strategies for Controlling Your Anger." rev. October 2011. Web May 16, 2013. http://www.apa.org/helpcenter/controlling-anger.aspx

Andersen, Peter. *The Complete Idiot's Guide to Body Language*. Indianapolis, IN: Alpha Books, 2004. Print.

Argyle, Michael. *Bodily Communication* (2nd ed.). Florence, KY: Routledge, 2010. Print.

Axtell, Roger. *Gestures: The Do's and Taboos of Body Language around the World*. Hoboken, NJ: Wiley, 1997. Print.

Bazelon, Emily. *Sticks and Stones: Defeating the Culture of Bullying and Rediscovering the Power of Character and Empathy*. New York: Random House, 2013. Print.

Berg, Rebecca. "Of Lice and Library: The Tale of an E-Mail." *Journal of Environmental Health*, January/February 2009: 8–9. Print.

Berry, J. "BackTalk: White Privilege in Library Land." *Library Journal*, June 15, 2004: 50. Print.

Bramson, Robert M. *Coping with Difficult People: The Proven-Effective Battle Plan that Has Helped Millions Deal with the Troublemakers*. New York: Dell, 1988. Print.

Brumley, Rebecca. *The Public Library Manager's Forms, Policies, and Procedures Handbook*. Chicago, IL: Neal-Schuman Publishers, 2004. Print.

Burgoon, Judee K. *Nonverbal Communications: The Unspoken Dialogue*. New York: McGraw Hill, 1995. Print.

Buschman, J., M. Rosenzweig, and E. Harger. (1994). "The Clear Imperative for Involvement: Librarians Must Address Social Issues." *American Libraries*. June 1994: 575–576. Print.

Bussert, L. "Americans' Tolerance of Racist Materials in Public Libraries Remained Steady Between 1976–2006." *Evidence Based Library and Information Practice*. 2012: 116–119. Print.

Cain, Susan. *Quiet: The Power of Introverts in a World that Can't Stop Talking*. New York: Random House, 2012. Print.

Carter, Rosalynn and Susan K. Galant. *Helping Someone with Mental Illness*. New York: Times Books, 1998. Print.

Chattoo, Calmer D. "The Problem Patron: Is There One in Your Library?" *Reference Librarian* 2002: 11–22. Print.

Cialdini, Robert B. *Influence: How and Why People Agree to Things*. New York: Quill, 1985. Print.

Cooley, Charles Horton. *Human Nature and the Social Order*. Memphis, TN: General Books LLC, 2010. Print.

Crowe, Sandra A. *Since Strangling isn't an Option: Dealing with Difficult People—Common Problems and Uncommon Solutions*. New York: Perigee Trade, 1999. Print.

Davitz, Joel Robert and Michael Beldoch. *The Communication of Emotional Meaning*. Westport, CT: Greenwood, 1976. Print.

Deep, Sam and Lyle Sussman. *What to Say to Get What You Want: Strong Words for 44 Challenging Types of Bosses, Employees, Coworkers, and Customers*. Reading, MA: Addison-Wesley, 1992. Print.

DeVito, Joseph A. and Dominic A. Infante. *Arguing Constructively*. Baltimore, MD: Waverly Press Inc., 1987. Print.

Dresser, Norine. *Multicultural Manners: Essential Rules of Etiquette for the 21st Century*. Hoboken, NJ: Wiley, 2005. Print.

Dreyfuss, Henry. *Symbol Sourcebook: An Authoritative Guide to International Graphic Symbols*. Hoboken, NJ: Wiley, 1994. Print.

Edwards, J. B., S. P. Edwards, and United Nations. *Beyond Article 19: Libraries and Social and Cultural Rights*. Duluth, MN: Library Juice Press, 2010. Print.

Egendorf, Laura K., ed. *Gangs: Opposing Viewpoints*. San Diego, CA: Greenhaven Press, 2001. Print.

Ellis, Albert. *How to Stubbornly Refuse to Make Yourself Miserable about Anything, Yes Anything*. New York: Citadel, 2006. Print.

Espelage, Dorothy L., Scott A. Napolitano, and Susan M. Swearer. *Bullying Prevention and Intervention: Realistic Strategies for Schools*. New York: The Guilford Press, 2009. Print.

Faber, Adele and Elaine Mazlish. *How to Talk so Kids Will Listen & Listen so Kids Will Talk*. New York: Avon, 1980. Print.

Foerstel, Herbert N. *Banned in the USA: A Reference Guide to Book Censorship in Schools and Public Libraries*. New York: Greenwood, 1994. Print.

Foerstel, Herbert N. *The Patriot Act: A Documentary and Reference Guide*. New York: Greenwood, 2007. Print.

Folger, Joseph P. *Working Through Conflict: Strategies for Relationships, Groups, and Organizations* (6th ed.). Columbus, OH: Allyn & Bacon, 2008. Print.

Friedman, Jenny and Jolene Roehlkepartain. *Doing Good Together: 101 Easy, Meaningful Service Projects for Families, Schools and Communities*. Minneapolis, MN: Free Spirit Publishing, 2010. Print.

Galant, Susan K. *Helping Someone with Mental Illness*. New York: Times Books, 1998. Print.

Gallagher, Richard S. *The Customer Service Survival Kit: What to Say to Defuse Even the Worst Customer Situations*. New York: AMACOM American Management Association, 2013. Print.

Glass, Lillian. *The Complete Idiot's Guide to Verbal Self-Defense*. New York: Alpha Books, 1999. Print.

Goleman, Daniel. *Emotional Intelligence: Why It Can Matter More Than I.Q.* (10th anniversary ed.). New York: Bantam, 2006. Print.

Grillo, T. and S. M. Wildman. "Obscuring the Importance of Race: The Implication of Making Comparisons between Racism and Sexism (Or Other-Isms)." *Duke Law Journal*. April 2, 1991: 397–412. Print.

Harmon, Charles and Michael Messina, eds. *Customer Service in Libraries: Best Practices*. New York: Scarecrow Press, 2013. Print.

Heinrichs, Jay. *Thank You for Arguing: What Aristotle, Lincoln, and Homer Simpson Can Teach Us About the Art of Persuasion*. New York: Three Rivers Press, 2007. Print.

Helper, Kim R. "Kreimer V Bureau of Police for Morristown: The Sterilization of the Local Library." Web June 23, 2013. http://www.law.stetson.edu/lawreview/media/kreimer-v-bureau-of-police-for-morristown-the-sterilization-of-the-local-library.pdf

Honma, T. "Trippin' Over the Color Line: The Invisibility of Race in Library and Information Studies." *InterActions: UCLA Journal of Education and Information 1*. 2005: 2. Print.

Horn, Sam. *Take the Bully by the Horns: Stop Unethical, Uncooperative, or Unpleasant People From Running and Ruining Your Life*. New York: St. Martin's Griffin, 2003. Print.

Isaacson, David. "No Problem with Problem Patrons." *Library Journal*. January 1, 2006: 68. Print.

Jerrard, Jane. *Crisis in Employment: a Librarian's Guide to Helping Job Seekers*. Chicago, IL: American Library Association, 2009. Print.

Kahn, Miriam B. *Disaster Response and Planning for Libraries* (3rd ed.). Chicago, IL: American Library Association, 2012. Print.

Kahn, Miriam B. *The Library Security and Safety Guide to Prevention, Planning, and Response* (3rd ed.). Chicago, IL: American Library Association, 2008. Print.

Kindler, Herbert S. *Managing Disagreement Constructively* (rev. ed.). Menlo Park, CA: Crisp Publications, 1997. Print.

Kreimer v. Bureau of Police, 958 F.2d 1242 (3d Cir. N.J. 1992). Web June 23, 2013. https://bulk.resource.org/courts.gov/c/F2/958/958.F2d.1242.91–5501.html?

Kunke, Elizabeth. *Body Language for Dummies*. Hoboken, NJ: Wiley, 2007. Print.

Lederer, William J. *Creating a Good Relationship*. New York: W.W. Norton Company Inc., 1984. Print.

Lemus, E. M. *Bullying 101: The Facts About Bullying*, Amazon Digital Services, Inc., 2013. Print.

Lloyd, J. D., ed. *Gangs*. San Diego, CA: Greenhaven Press, 2002. Print

Mayo Clinic. "Answers." Web May 31, 2013. http://www.mayoclinic.com

McCook, K. de la Peña and K. J Phenix. "Public Libraries and Human Rights." *Public Library Quarterly 25 (1)*. 2006: 57–73. Print.

McQuade III, Samuel C. *Cyber Bullying: Protecting Kids and Adults from Online Bullies*. Santa Barbara, CA: Praeger, 2009. Print.

Minow, Mary. "Policy Writing—The Next Level: Making Sure Your Policies are Legally Enforceable—Key Resources." Web June 23, 2013. http://www.librarylaw.com/librarycases.doc

Minow, Mary. "Will it hold up in Court? Writing Legally Enforceable Library Policies." Web June 23, 2013. http://lss.njstatelib.org/ldb_files/imported/Trustees/Trustee_Institute/EnforceablePolicies.ppt#951,1,Slide 1

Mitnick, Kevin. "Should We Fear Hackers? Intention is at the Heart of this Discussion." *The Guardian*. February 22, 2000: n.p. Print.

Morden, Peter A. and Diane M. Samdahl. *The Diverse Worlds of Unemployed Adults: Consequences for Leisure, Lifestyle and Well-Being*. New York: Wilfrid Laurier University Press, 2004. Print.

Mosley, Shelley, Anna Caggiano, and John Charles. "The 'Self-Weeding' Collection: The Ongoing Problem of Library Theft, and How to Fight Back." *Library Journal*. October 15, 1996: 38+. Print.

National Alliance on Mental Illness. "What Is Mental Illness?" Web June 6, 2013. http://www.nami.org

National Coalition for the Homeless. NCH Fact Sheet #5, "Mental Illness and Homelessness." Web May 31, 2013. http://www.nationalhomeless.org

National Gang Center. Web May 23, 2013. http://www.nationalgangcenter.gov

National Resource Directory: Homeless Assistance. Web May 31, 2013. www.nrd.gov/homeless_assistance

Navarro, Joe and Marvin Karlins. *What Every BODY is Saying: An Ex-FBI Agent's Guide to Speed-Reading People*. New York: William Morrow Paperbacks, 2008. Print.

New York Public Library. *Turn It Up @ the Library: Racist Slurs and Homophobia: A Podcast Made by Teens at the 125th Street Branch of the New York Public Library*. Web January 2008.

Nhat Hanh, Thich. *Keeping the Peace: Mindfulness and Public Service*. Berkeley, CA: Parallax Press, 2005. Print.

Nye, Valerie and Kathy Barco. *True Stories of Censorship Battles in America's Libraries*. Chicago, IL: American Library Association, 2012. Print.

Office of Juvenile Justice and Delinquency Prevention. Web May 23, 2013. http://www.ojjdp.gov/programs/antigang

Peterson, L. "Alternative Perspectives in Library and Information Science: Issues of Race." *Journal of Education for Library and Information Science*. Spring 1996: 163–174. Print.

Psychology Today. *Psych Basics: Bullying, "Understanding Bullying."* Web May 16, 2003. http://www.psychologytoday.com/basics/bullying

Raber, D. "ACONDA and ANACONDA: Social Change, Social Responsibility, and Librarianship." *Library Trends*. 2007: 675–697. Print.

Robbins, Louise. *Censorship and the American Library: The American Library Association's Response to Threats to Intellectual Freedom*. Santa Barbara, CA: Praeger, 1996. Print.

Robbins, Louise. *The Dismissal of Miss Ruth Brown: Civil Rights, Censorship, and the American Library*. Santa Barbara, CA: Praeger, 2001. Print.

Roleff, Tamara L., ed. *Hate Crimes*. San Diego, CA: Greenhaven Press, 2001. Print.

Russell, James A. and Jose Miguel Fernandez-Dols. *The Psychology of Facial Expression*. New York: Cambridge University Press, 1997. Print.

Samek, T. *Intellectual Freedom and Social Responsibility in American Librarianship*. Jefferson, NC: McFarland & Company, Inc., Publishers, 2001. Print.

Sarkodie-Mensah, Kwasi, ed. *Helping the Difficult Library Patron*. New York: Routledge, 2002. Print.

Schacter, Daniel L. and Daniel M. Wegner. *Psychology* (2nd ed.). New York: Worth Publishers, 2010. Print.

Schull, Diantha Dow. *50+ Library Services: Innovation in Action*. Chicago, IL: American Library Association, 2013. Print.

Shimomura, Tsutomo and John Markoff. *Takedown: The Pursuit and Capture of Kevin Mitnick, America's Most Wanted Computer Outlaw—By the Man Who Did It*. London: Voice, 1996. Print.

Shuman, Bruce A. *Library Security and Safety Handbook: Prevention, Policies, and Procedures*. Chicago, IL: American Library Association, 1999. Print.

Steil, Lyman K. *Effective Listening: Key to Your Success*. Boston, MA: Addison-Wesley, 1985. Print.

Stewart, Lea P., et al. *Communication and Gender* (4th ed.). New York: Allyn & Bacon, 2002. Print.

Switzer, Teri R. *Safe at Work? Library Security and Safety Issues*. Lanham, MD: Scarecrow Press, 1999. Print.

Tannen, Deborah. *You Just Don't Understand: Women and Men in Conversation*. New York: Harper, 2001. Print.

Taylor, Paul. *Hackers: Crime and the Digital Sublime*. New York: Routledge, 1999. Print.

Uhl, Arlene Matthews. *The Complete Idiot's Guide to Coping with Difficult People*. New York: Alpha, 2007. Print.

United States. Department of Health & Human Resources. *Stopbullying.gov*. Web May 16, 2013. http://www.stopbullying.gov

United States. Department of Health & Human Resources. "Alcoholism." Web May 13, 2013. http://search.nih.gov/search?utf8=%E2%9C%93&affiliate=nih&query=ALCOHOLISM

United States.. Department of Health and Human Services. "Homelessness." Web May 23, 2013. http://www.hhs.gov/homeless/

United States Office of Special Counsel. "Frequently Asked Questions." Web May 31, 2013. http://www.osc.gov/haFederalfaq.htm

United States Department of Housing and Urban Development. "Homelessness Resource Exchange." Web May 23, 2013. http://www.hudhre.info

United States Department of Labor. "Occupational Safety and Health Administration." *Workers Rights*. Web May 16, 2013. http://www.osha.gov/Publications/osha3021.pdf

United States Interagency Council on Homelessness. "Resources." Web May 23, 2013. http://www.usich.gov/usich_resources

United States Office of Special Counsel. "Frequently Asked Questions." Web May 31, 2013. http://www.osc.gov/haFederalfaq.htm

Weissman, Jerry. *In the Line of Fire: How to Handle Tough Questions When it Counts*. Upper Saddle River, NJ: Pearson Prentice Hall, 2005. Print.

Whitaker, Todd and Fiore, Douglas. *Dealing with Difficult Parents and With Parents in Difficult Situations*. New York: Eye on Education, 2001. Print.

Williams, Dian L. *Understanding the Arsonist: From Assessment to Confession* (2nd ed.). Tucson, AZ: Lawyers and Judges Publishing, 2013. Print.

Williams, Stanley Tookie. *Gangs and Weapons*. New York: Rosen Pub. Group, 1996. Print.

INDEX

ABOUT THE AUTHORS

Retired library manager SHELLEY E. MOSLEY coauthored *Romance Today: An A-to-Z Guide to Contemporary American Romance Writers*; *The Suffragists in Literature for Youth: The Fight for the Vote*; and *The Complete Idiot's Guide to the Ultimate Reading List*. She and Dennis Tucker coauthored *Crash Course in Library Supervision: Meeting the Key Players*. She has written hundreds of articles and reviews for professional journals and is a long-time contributor to *What Do I Read Next?* and NoveList. Mosley is enjoying her so-called "retirement" by writing full-time.

DENNIS C. TUCKER is Reference/Adult Programming Librarian for the Stockton–San Joaquin County Public Library in Stockton, California. He holds a master of arts in library science from the University of Missouri–Columbia, a master of arts in teaching from Southeast Missouri State University, and a PhD from the Graduate Theological Foundation. He and Shelley Mosley are the coauthors of *Crash Course in Library Supervision: Meeting the Key Players*.

SANDRA VAN WINKLE coauthored *Romance Today: An A-Z Guide to Contemporary American Romance Writers* and *The Complete Idiot's Guide to the Ultimate Reading List*. She also contributes to *What Do I Read Next?* Van Winkle specializes in technical writing, and is an experienced grant writer. She has library experience and received her bachelor of arts degree in public administration from Ottawa University.

45.00   5/9/14

LONGWOOD PUBLIC LIBRARY
800 Middle Country Road
Middle Island, NY 11953
(631) 924-6400
longwoodlibrary.org

LIBRARY HOURS

Monday-Friday	9:30 a.m. - 9:00 p.m.
Saturday	9:30 a.m. - 5:00 p.m.
Sunday (Sept-June)	1:00 p.m. - 5:00 p.m.